The Lives of Transgender People

THE LIVES OF

TRANSGENDER PEOPLE

Genny Beemyn and Susan Rankin

COLUMBIA UNIVERSITY PRESS

NEW YORK

Columbia University Press
Publishers Since 1893
New York   Chichester, West Sussex
Copyright © 2011 Columbia University Press
All rights reserved

Library of Congress Cataloging-in-Publication Data
Beemyn, Genny.
The lives of transgender people / Genny Beemyn and Susan Rankin.
p. cm.
Includes bibliographical references and index.
ISBN 978-0-231-14306-6 (cloth : alk. paper) —
ISBN 978-0-231-14307-3 (pbk. : alk. paper) —
ISBN 978-0-231-51261-9 (e-book)
1. Transgender people—United States. 2. Transgender youth—United
States. 3. Gender identity—United States. I. Rankin, Susan. II. Title.
HQ77.95.U6.B44 2011
306.76'80973—dc23
2011025083

Casebound editions of Columbia University Press books are printed on
permanent and durable acid-free paper.
Printed in the United States of America
c 10 9 8 7 6 5 4 3 2
p 10 9 8 7 6 5
References to Internet Web sites (URLs) were accurate at the time of
writing. Neither the author nor Columbia University Press is responsible
for Web sites that may have expired or changed since the book was
prepared.

CONTENTS

FOREWORD

Shannon Minter

This groundbreaking study by Genny Beemyn and Sue Rankin is the first to examine the full diversity of the transgender community—not only those who are transsexual but also the growing number of individuals who identify their genders in nonbinary ways. Through surveys and interviews with a huge sampling of transgender people from across the country, it is the first major study to combine methodological rigor with an insider's grasp of the nuances and complexities of transgender lives. As a transgender attorney who has spent the last seventeen years advocating for transgender people, I have often wished for a book like this on my shelf.

With their fresh and sophisticated approach, the authors have uncovered a treasure trove of eye-opening data. They present vital new information about how transgender people discover their identities, how they forge viable life paths even in the face of great hostility, and how those life paths are changing dramatically for young people coming of age in a world that has been transformed by the Internet and other new social media. This information is essential for policy makers seeking to protect and include transgender youth in schools and other settings.

Beemyn and Rankin bring impressive credentials to this project. Beemyn is a national expert on how to develop and implement supportive policies for transgender students in higher education. Rankin is a leading researcher on campus climate and diversity issues, with an unparalleled record of scholarship about discrimination against lesbian, gay, bisexual, and transgender people in college and university settings. Their collaboration has set a new benchmark for research in this area.

This study is the first to explore the process of identity development in different transgender groups and across different generations of transgender people. Prior studies in this field have been based on samples that were limited by size, geography, age, race, gender, and narrow definitions of who is counted as transgender. To ensure a more representative view, Beemyn and Rankin recruited a large, diverse sample of transgender people from across the country. They surveyed 3,474 participants by drawing on contacts with transgender groups and individuals from throughout the United States. In addition, they conducted interviews with 419 of the survey respondents.

Beemyn and Rankin also break new ground in their approach to determining who qualifies as transgender for purposes of empirical research. Past studies of transgender people have generally failed to include people with nonbinary identities, perhaps in part because the task of definition is so daunting. Beemyn and Rankin recognized that attempting to define who counts as transgender would hinder, rather than advance, their ability to study a community in which new identities are rapidly emerging. As a result, this is the first large-scale study that includes "not just MTF and FTM individuals and cross-dressers but also genderqueers, androgynes, bigenders, third genders, transgenderists, and other transgender individuals who describe their genders in nonbinary ways."

To cast the widest possible net, Beemyn and Rankin permitted survey participants to self-identify and specifically explained that the survey included those who do not identify simply as either men or women. The resulting diversity was startling. The authors report that "the 257 participants who characterized themselves as 'other' (rather than female, male, or transgender) used 119 additional descriptors for themselves, of which 101 were unique responses." For example, participants described themselves as "fluid," "neutral," "queer," "two-spirit," "somewhere between transsexual and cross-dresser," "FTM TG stone butch drag king," and "no easy definition, some other kind of man."

In the hands of less savvy researchers, this proliferation of terms and identities might have defied meaningful analysis. But Beemyn and Rankin handle this potential dilemma masterfully, elegantly drawing out key threads. They propose a useful new term, "different-gender," to describe those who do not identify as men or women. Thus, as counterparts to the terms "female-to-male transsexual" and "male-to-female transsexual," they employ the terms "female-to-different-gender" and "male-to-different-gender" in describing individuals who do not identify with their assigned gender yet who are not transsexual. These new terms are a welcome scholarly addition to the more colloquial term "genderqueer."

Beemyn and Rankin's new framework and terms also enable them to examine important gendered differences among those who do not identify as either male or female. For example, the study found that the vast majority of the respondents who identify as something other than male or female were assigned female at birth, which may reflect "the overall greater leeway in gender expression experienced by the respondents who were raised as women."

The study also found important differences between cross-dressers and individuals who identify as some type of male-to-different-gender identity (such as "genderqueer," "gender fluid," "bigendered," "third gendered," "androgynous," or "boi"). Those who self-identified as cross-dressers often saw themselves as "having a second, female self that is separate from their male gender identity." In contrast, those who identified as male-to-different-gender saw themselves "in ways that challenge conventional static, binary constructions of gender." In addition, whereas survey respondents who self-identified as cross-dressers were substantially older on average than the other transgender people surveyed, those who described their gender in nonbinary terms were substantially younger. Based on this trend, the authors suggest that "fewer young people today are choosing to refer to themselves as cross-dressers" and that the term "cross-dresser" itself may be passing out of common usage.

The study also uncovered striking patterns in how transgender identity develops in different groups within the transgender community. For example, most of the participants reported feeling "different" from other children from an early age. But the respondents' experiences of how they responded to those childhood feelings of difference diverged sharply based on whether they were assigned female or male at birth. More than 80 percent of the female-to-male participants (FTMs or transsexual men) were able to express their internal feelings of masculinity as children "by taking on traditionally male roles in play and in relationships with other children." In contrast, only 37 percent of the male-to-female participants (MTFs or transsexual women) dared to express a sustained interest in feminine activities or clothing as children. Most who did were physically or sexually assaulted, sent to therapists, or physically or emotionally abused by their families.

The study also found that transsexual men were more likely to have been traumatized by the experience of puberty than transsexual women—a fascinating discovery that has not previously been documented. After enjoying greater latitude to express their gender identities as children, many FTMs lost that freedom when they entered adolescence and faced the more rigid gender norms imposed on young women. "With the onset of menstruation and breast development," many FTM participants were devastated that they "no longer fit in as just 'one of the boys' . . . ; as the line between male and female became more strictly drawn, these individuals realized that they were being placed on the 'wrong' side." In contrast, many transsexual women were already accustomed to hiding and suppressing their identities because of the punishment inflicted on feminine boys.

As adults, transsexual women were also considerably more likely than transsexual men to try to hide or suppress their transgender identities by conforming to traditional gender roles. Many of the transsexual women in the study reported seeking out hypermasculine occupations, such as military service or becoming husbands and fathers, in an effort to disguise or change their internal feelings. Only when they faced a life crisis were they compelled to give up that struggle, come to terms with their female identities, and begin to live as women.

In contrast, few FTM interviewees tried to adopt conventionally feminine gender roles as adults; yet many identified as lesbians for an extended period before realizing that gender transition was an option. In fact, "nearly half of the FTM people (as compared with about a quarter of the MTF people) reported initially lacking information about others like themselves—including knowledge that transitioning was possible." Thus, whereas many older MTFs were aware they could transition but still struggled to suppress their female identities until a life crisis propelled them forward, a key developmental milestone for many older FTMs was discovering transition as an option and meeting other transsexual men. For many, meeting other FTMs sparked a process of self-recognition, eventually allowing them to self-identify as transsexual and live as men.

It is notable that at least some of these gendered differences in the lives of transgender people may be diminishing because of the Internet, which has dramatically increased access to information for all sorts of elsewhere marginalized subcultures. Increasingly, transgender individuals of all types are likely to have information and contact with other transgender people at a much earlier age. Regardless of their assigned gender at birth, "the younger the [study] participant, the more likely that person was to have had access to transgender people and resources at a young age." More than two-thirds of the eighteen- to twenty-two-year-olds surveyed knew other transgender people by the time they came out as transgender, compared with only about a third of the respondents in their forties and a quarter of those fifty and older. In another study cited by the authors, a remarkable 54 percent of self-identified transgender youth in New York City reported socializing with other transgender people on a daily basis.

The study also found that transgender individuals are coming out at increasingly younger ages. Only four of the twenty-one interviewees between eighteen and twenty-one years old reported trying to deny or suppress their sense of gender difference as children or adolescents. Most learned about the possibility of gender transition and about the range of transgender identities at a relatively early age, as adolescents or even as children. Having that information enabled them to understand their internal feelings of gender difference and come to terms with their transgender identities without years of confusion, concealment, or shame. This data confirms the anecdotal experience of many parents, teachers, and school administrators, who report increasing numbers of children and youth who are self-identifying as transgender and as gender nonconforming.

Yet even in this new world of vastly increased access to information, most of the college-aged participants went through a process of exploration before settling into an identity that felt most comfortable. Unlike many of the older participants, who "seemed to use other identities as a means to avoid facing their 'true' selves, sometimes for years or decades," most younger participants "experimented relatively briefly with different identities before arriving at one that felt right to them." For example, many of the younger female-assigned participants identified as butch lesbians or as genderqueer before coming out as transsexual men. But unlike many of the older FTMs, they did so only briefly and not for an extended period.

As an FTM who struggled to live as a lesbian for many years before coming out as transsexual, I am fascinated by the stories of younger transsexual men who are able to bypass those years of internal struggle and find their path more directly. It is intriguing, and even a little poignant, to imagine a future in which most transsexual men will no longer have the experience of identifying as lesbians for any significant period. But it is also exciting to realize that we are on the brink of a world in which transgender children and youth can be embraced and supported for who they are.

Unfortunately, the greater visibility of transgender issues has not brought an end to gender-based harassment and discrimination. More than a quarter of the respondents surveyed had experienced harassment because of their gender identity or expression within the past year. Nearly one in five had lost a job or been denied employment or advancement as a result of being transgender. Many reported sometimes or often hiding their gender identity in an effort to avoid violence or discrimination. In fact, the greater visibility of transgender youth has likely increased their exposure to mistreatment in some respects. Younger participants in the study reported markedly higher levels of harassment because of their gender identity or expression within the previous year.

At the same time, transgender youth have made incredible progress by coming out. In Massachusetts, a transgender girl won a landmark legal ruling that her high school must permit her to wear female clothing. The court refused to "allow the stifling of plaintiff's selfhood merely because it causes some members of the community discomfort. . . . Defendants are essentially prohibiting the plaintiff from expressing her gender identity and, thus, her quintessence."[1] In Mississippi, Ceara Sturgis courageously battled her school for the right to wear a tuxedo in her senior yearbook photo. And in Washington, DC, Kye Allums became the first NCAA basketball player to publicly identify as a transsexual man, paving the way for countless other transgender athletes.

Beemyn and Rankin have also made an important contribution to scholarship on transgender identity by beginning to document how other facets of a person's identity, when combined with being transgender, affect life experiences. For example, in addition to the study's findings on age, Beemyn and Rankin found that transgender people who identified as heterosexual were less likely to report harassment than transgender people of other sexual orientations. Transgender people of color were more likely to face harassment, with American Indian respondents reporting the highest rates.

Like the other information presented in this groundbreaking study, the findings on race, sexual orientation, age, and other factors represent milestones in our understanding of the experiences of transgender people. But even more importantly, these findings represent a critical beginning: they provoke new questions and push us further along the path to understanding more fully, and thus better serving, every person in the multiple communities that make up the entire spectrum of transgender lives.

ACKNOWLEDGMENTS

Although we are the authors of this book, it has been influenced by and draws its power from an amazing group of people—colleagues, students, scholars, transgender activists, and others—with whom we have had the pleasure of collaborating over the years. We especially express our appreciation to our colleagues and friends for their supporting the pursuit of our passion; to the Consortium of Higher Education LGBT Resource Professionals, which inspires and energizes us; and to our students, who continually challenge us to "see" beyond our lens. Genny would also like to acknowledge the tremendous support ze received from hir mother, Carol, Sara, Ilana, Jessica, Laura, and most especially Sue in persevering to complete the book. Sue would also like to express her deep gratitude to Alex and Genevieve for their assistance in conducting the statistical analyses; to Aaron and Mara for their friendship and tireless work in the transgender community; to her family for not allowing her to take herself too seriously; and to her partner, Allison, whose love and sense of humor sustained her and whose strength of soul continually uplifts her. Thank you all!

We would also like to thank the many transgender groups that publicized our research to their members as well as the venues that gave us the opportunity to present our findings and discuss our analysis, including Nancy Nangeroni and Gordene MacKenzie's GenderTalk Radio and the National Gay and Lesbian Task Force's Creating Change Conference. We also greatly appreciate Lauren Dockett and Columbia University Press for not giving up on us when we missed deadline after deadline. We hope it was worth the wait.

Finally and most importantly, we would like to express our deep gratitude to the transgender people who took the time to complete the survey, especially the individuals who agreed to a follow-up interview and/or to be pictured in the book. The powerful and moving stories that you shared were an ongoing source of inspiration and repeatedly demonstrated to us the importance of a book on the lives of transgender people.

The Lives of Transgender People

INTRODUCTION

I always liked playing "dress-up"—in secret—but wrote it off as a game until I had an epiphany when I was seventeen, at which point I realized there was more to it than that. But I didn't know there was a term for it, nor that others felt the same way. Once I heard the term "transvestite" I thought that must be what I was. Nowadays I prefer the term "cross-dresser" . . . [but] it doesn't really seem to cover it. . . . There is more to it for me than just the dressing. The vocabulary describing us is lacking.

—GLORIA[1]

I do not try to fit a box; I am simply me.

—KIM L.

People who do not identify entirely or at all with the gender assigned to them at birth have steadily achieved greater recognition over the past century. They include male-to-female (MTF) transsexuals (individuals assigned male at birth who identify as and often seek to transition to female), female-to-male (FTM) transsexuals (individuals assigned female at birth who identify as and often seek to transition to male), cross-dressers (individuals who present at least part time as a gender different from the one assigned to them at birth), drag kings and drag queens (individuals who cross-dress in traditionally masculine and feminine ways, respectively, mainly for performance), genderqueers (individuals who identify as a different gender or as somewhere in between male and female), bigenders (individuals who identify as both male and female), and androgynes (individuals who identify as androgynous). The increasing visibility of what has become known as the transgender community is reflected in the rapidly growing body of literature that examines their lives.

But for all the studies conducted involving transgender people, there has not been a large-scale empirical work that considers the diversity of experiences that fall under the term "transgender." As college administrators and educators, we have been particularly concerned by the absence of studies that compare the identity development processes of different transgender groups and different generations of transgender people. Such research can lead to a much better understanding of the lives of transgender people, and it is for this reason that we wrote this book.

DEVELOPMENT OF TRANSGENDER STUDIES

Since German physician Magnus Hirschfeld (1910/1991) coined the term "transvestites" in 1910 to describe individuals who are more comfortable in clothing of a gender different than their birth gender, many researchers and medical professionals have sought to understand this population. The distinction made between cross-dressers and transsexual people, first popularized by U.S. endocrinologist Harry Benjamin (1966), sparked further interest in cross-gender identities. Most of the empirical research since then has focused on a specific transgender group or occasionally compared two groups. The earliest large-sample studies of transgender communities in the 1960s and early 1970s (Prince 1962; Prince & Bentler 1972) involved female-presenting cross-dressers because—since the "transvestite" clubs and periodicals of the time had significant memberships and readerships—they were the most accessible transgender group.

Although the findings of these studies indicate that a number of the individuals associated with "transvestite" clubs were transsexual, most of these groups sought to exclude them and draw a sharp distinction between wanting to *appear as* a woman and wanting to *be* a woman. As a result, researchers who sought to study transsexual people turned to the patients of the growing number of gender identity clinics in the late 1960s and 1970s. For example, Neil Buhrich and Neil McConaghy (1977, 1978, 1979) compared members of an Australian "transvestite" club to transsexual people seeking treatment at one of the country's gender identity clinics as well as to a gay control group, and Elizabeth McCauley and Anke Ehrhardt (1977) compared FTM individuals who sought services at a U.S. psychoendocrinology clinic to volunteers from a local lesbian group.

As transsexual groups became more numerous in the 1980s and 1990s and as many exclusively "transvestite" clubs began to welcome transsexual individuals, researchers were able to study nonclinical populations of both transsexual people and "transvestites" (Bolin 1988; Buhrich & Beaumont 1981; Bullough, Bullough, & Smith 1983; Docter 1988; Docter & Fleming 1993; Gagné, Tewksbury, & McGaughey 1997; Hogan-Finlay, Spanos, & Jones 1997; Schott 1995; Talamini 1982). More recent research has further depathologized female-presenting cross-dressers by no longer describing them as "transvestites" (Bullough & Bullough 1997; Rudd 1999) and has focused on the experiences of FTM individuals (Devor 1997a, 1997b; Ringo 2002; Rubin 2003). Other works published in the last few years have focused on transgender children (Brill & Pepper 2008), teens (Beam 2007), and college students (Bilodeau 2009) and on the sexual orientation of MTF transgender people (Samons 2009).

None of these studies consider all transgender people—not just MTF and FTM individuals and cross-dressers but also genderqueers, androgynes, bigenders, third genders, transgenderists, and other transgender individuals who describe their genders in nonbinary ways. Except for Lori Girshick's *Transgender Voices* (2008), the few studies that have included a broad transgender sample either did not ask how people specifically identified (McKinney 2005; Rankin 2003) or did not use this data extensively in their analysis (Grossman & D'Augelli 2006; Lombardi, Wilchins, Priesing, & Malouf 2001).

The failure of research to include the experiences of transgender people with nonbinary identities is not surprising given that, until the 1990s and early 2000s, most transgender groups operated from a narrow gender framework. The first "transvestite" clubs were founded by heterosexual male cross-dressers who excluded MTF individuals and gay and openly bisexual cross-dressers—in part to allay the fears of many of their female partners that they were going to leave them to be with a man or to "become" a woman. Many cross-dressing groups broke away from this paradigm in the 1980s and began to admit transsexual members. However, some of the organizations still maintained a strict binary understanding of gender and gender identities. Cultural anthropologist Anne Bolin (1988) reported that potential members of a midwestern support group in the early 1980s had to announce whether they were cross-dressers or MTF individuals, according to whether they desired gender reassignment/confirmation surgery, and to follow the social script for that identity. Revisiting the group about a decade later, Bolin (1994) found that members accepted greater gender diversity; in particular, the MTF participants had become more welcoming of transsexual women who did not pursue surgery.

Still, being more open does not necessarily mean that trans-gender groups today are inclusive of all gender-nonconforming people. In the early 2000s, when one of us sought to participate in a local transgender organization that consisted largely of cross-dressers and MTF individuals in their forties, fifties, and sixties, many members considered "ze"[2] simply an ally, even though ze openly identified as genderqueer. Only after ze had coordinated a number of transgender events, changed ze's name, and began facial hair removal did some leaders of the transgender community seem to accept ze as "one of us." This anecdote reflects an age division in some transgender communities between older individuals, who came of age when the only viable options were identifying as a transsexual or a cross-dresser, and younger people, who today live in a world in which it is common to identify outside of binary gender categories. For researchers who rely on well-established local transgender groups for survey samples, this age divide means that they will likely exclude many younger people and, as a result, describe only a narrow range of transgender identities in their work.

(RE)DEFINING TRANSGENDER EXPERIENCES

For much of the twentieth century, the literature on cross-dressers, transsexual people, and other gender-diverse individuals was reductive and pathologizing. Even though Hirschfeld (1910/1991) found that "transvestites" could be men or women, could identify as any sexual orientation (most of his study participants were behaviorally heterosexual), and differed from fetishists, psychoanalysts such as Wilhelm Stekel (1930) subsequently characterized "transvestites" as men who were "latent homosexuals" or in denial about their homosexuality. By the 1970s, studies of "transvestites" (e.g., Prince & Bentler 1972; Stoller 1971) went to the opposite extreme, arguing that they were largely or exclusively heterosexual men and often linking cross-dressing to fetishism. This understanding of "transvestism" was codified into the third (1980) edition of the American Psychiatric Association's *Diagnostic and Statistical Manual of Mental Disorders (DSM)*. The "disorder" was renamed "transvestic fetishism" in subsequent editions (1987, 1994, 2000) and adopted as a framework by some researchers (Docter 1988) despite criticism from activists (GID Reform Advocates 2004) and other scholars (Bullough & Bullough 1993). Transsexuality, since being identified as a separate phenomenon from "transvestitism," has also been considered a mental illness by some researchers (Bailey 2003; Blanchard 2000) and has likewise been included in the *DSM* since 1980. Transsexuality remains in the manual today (American Psychiatric Association 2000) as "Gender Identity Disorder," and editors of the *DSM*'s next edition, due to be published in 2013, have proposed that the diagnosis remain but be renamed "Gender Incongruence" (American Psychiatric Association 2010).

Our approach in undertaking this research was that cross-dressing, transsexuality, and other transgender identities are no less "natural" or "legitimate" than the dominant gender categories of women and men. Detractors may contend that we lack adequate critical distance or are biased by virtue of our membership in transgender/queer communities, yet we feel that our positions give us insights that have been absent from much of the literature on transgender lives, which has largely been written by cisgender[3] (i.e., nontransgender) researchers. Our connections to the communities that we are studying also enabled us to involve many transgender people in the research who otherwise would have been reluctant to participate for fear of further mistreatment by academics. To a great extent, our "insider" status enabled us to conduct one of the largest surveys to date of transgender people in the United States.

Our research also differs from many previous studies in that we did not seek to define who qualified to be counted as transgender. All people living in the United States who currently identify as transgender or gender nonconforming in some way or who have identified as transgender in the past (i.e., FTM and MTF individuals who have transitioned and no longer consider themselves transgender) were encouraged to participate. We also did not exclude respondents who did not fit the definitions commonly used for transgender people in the psychological literature, such as transsexual individuals who do not transition completely or at all, female-presenting cross-dressers who have never been sexually stimulated by their cross-dressing or who are attracted to men, and gender-nonconforming individuals who challenge traditional transgender categories.

In addition, we have sought to use inclusive language when describing transgender communities. Unless otherwise indicated, we will be using the word "transgender" as a general term for all individuals whose gender histories cannot be described as simply female or male, even if they now identify and express themselves as strictly female or male. Although some of the older cross-dressers who participated in our research self-identified as "transvestites," most members of this group referred to themselves using the more inclusive and less clinical term "cross-dressers." We will do likewise and will use "transvestite" only when quoting individual respondents or researchers.

Finally, we do not distinguish between what have been called "primary transsexuals" (typically MTF individuals with lifelong cross-gender identities) and "secondary transsexuals" (those who often identified as cross-dressers or as gay men before recognizing themselves as transsexuals). Although this division is common in clinically oriented texts (Docter 1988; Freund, Steiner, & Chan 1982; Person & Ovesey 1974a, 1974b; Stoller 1985), we find such a hierarchy to be unnecessarily judgmental and of little value: the distinction seems more a function of exposure to information and to other transsexual individuals than of any actual psychological difference. Many of the older MTF participants in our research believed they were cross-dressers until they learned, often through the Internet, about transsexuality and the existence of other people like themselves. In contrast, few of the younger MTF respondents, who grew up in an online world, ever identified themselves as cross-dressers. Another weakness of the studies that differentiate between primary and secondary transsexualism is that, like most of the psychological literature on transgender people, these works largely ignore the experiences of FTM individuals.

METHODS

The survey that serves as the basis for this book was sparked by previous research we conducted involving transgender college students (Beemyn 2003; Rankin 2003). Our work revealed the absence of models of identity formation that address the experiences of multiple segments of the transgender community, so we decided to develop such a model. We wanted to consider the developmental experiences of all types of people in the United States who self-identify as transgender or who did so in the past, such as FTM and MTF individuals who have transitioned and no longer consider themselves transgender.

To better understand the respondents' experiences, we employed a mixed methods design[4] and triangulated between the three methods (survey, in-person and phone interviews, and e-mail interviews). The survey tool provided quantitative data and the means to reach the largest pool of potential participants. The e-mail, phone, and face-to-face interviews gave "voice" to the data. To derive theory from the material, all interviews were analyzed using a constant comparative method (Glaser & Strauss 1967). As described by Katherine Hiestand and Heidi Levitt (2005), the process involves breaking down each of the interview transcripts into units that communicate one main idea and assigning each unit a label that represents that idea. Each label is compared with the other labels for the purpose of grouping them into categories, and these categories are then further compared with each other to create main categories that capture a critical concept. These concepts formed the basis for the different transgender life events discussed in chapter 4.

Our own life experiences and understandings of sex-gender systems informed and contextualized our methods of conducting this study. We are both U.S. citizens of European American descent, have earned advanced degrees and worked for many years in higher education, and self-identify as queer. Genny was assigned male at birth but identifies more as female and describes hirself as genderqueer. Sue was born and identifies as female; that is, ze is cisgender and does not identify as transgender. Although Sue may not conform to many sex-gender norms, hir gender assigned at birth has coincided with hir gender identity/expression over the course of hir life. Given the privileges associated with being cisgender in our society, it is with particular care and thoughtfulness that Sue approaches discussions of gender diversity.

This book is not written in a particular methodological tradition; nor is our research limited solely to quantitative, qualitative, or rhetorical evidence. Our work is interdisciplinary, not only in the conventional academic sense of drawing from many different disciplines but also in terms of our experiences as researchers and educators: collecting data, analyzing interviews, and teaching about social justice and the intersections of identity. Our position is that fostering equality for transgender people requires the commitment of people of all gender identities and expressions.

THE SURVEY

Taking into consideration the findings of previous studies of transgender people (Bolin 1988; Bullough & Bullough 1993; Devor 1997a; Rubin 2003) and models of sexual identity development (D'Augelli 1994a; Hiestand & Levitt 2005; Troiden 1989), we constructed an anonymous, forty-one-question, online survey (appendix A). The survey also provided space for respondents to provide additional comments. The participants were asked to provide information about their development as transgender individuals, their personal experiences, and other demographic information. All surveys were entered into a secure database and tabulated for analysis.

SAMPLING

The project proposal, including the survey instrument, was reviewed and approved in November 2006 by the Institutional Review Boards for Human Subjects Research of the authors' institutions at the time (Pennsylvania State University and Ohio State University). The proposal indicated that the collection and analysis of the data would ensure participant anonymity. The final Web-based survey was distributed from November 2005 through February 2006. Given the difficulty of identifying significant numbers of transgender people, the authors e-mailed information about the project and an invitation to participate to transgender listservs, support groups that had an online presence, public transgender figures, and people who had personal profiles on transgender websites. An attempt was made to contact transgender individuals and groups in all fifty states. People and organizations that agreed to assist with the project were subsequently sent the web link to the survey. At the end of the survey, individuals were invited to participate in a follow-up interview by contacting one of the authors.

THE INTERVIEWS

So that participants could discuss their life histories in greater detail, we conducted follow-up interviews by e-mail, by phone, and in person. The interview questions were developed based on the results of the survey and on Richard Troiden's model of lesbian and gay identity formation (1989). The interviewees were told that the interviewer would be taking notes during the interview and were given a description of the means by which confidentiality would be ensured in the transcription and analysis of the interview. Any questions that the interviewees had were also answered. The participants engaged in a semistructured, open-ended interview covering such topics as when they first felt gender different, the process by which they came to identify as transgender, and their experiences with friends, family, and community (see appendix B for the interview protocol). The interviewees decided whether their first name or a pseudonym of their choosing would be used in the study.

DATA ANALYSIS

The quantitative data was cleaned and the variables constructed via SPSS 17. Descriptive statistics were provided, and several cross-tabulations were performed. The relevant data are the frequencies with which transgender people who exhibit varying demographic characteristics rated their experiences and perceptions—all nominal-level data. Hence when statistical comparisons are made, chi-square tests of significance were used. Chi-square tests are appropriate because we compared expected with observed frequencies within response categories.

To determine the four "transgender variables" (female-to-male/transgender, male-to-female/transgender, female-to-different-gender, and male-to-different-gender) through which many comparisons were made, a multivariate analysis of variance (MANOVA), an analysis of variance (ANOVA), and binary logistic regression were used to examine whether differences existed between groups in terms of when they began to identify as transgender.[5] The MANOVAs, as opposed to separate ANOVAs, were used to analyze the group of age-related questions as well as questions describing the respondents' level of "outness" in various situations. This approach allowed us to control for estimation errors that stem from dependent variables being correlated with each other. Because the assumption of homogeneity of variance was not met, Dunnett's T3 test was used to compare the means of different groups. Based on this analysis, participants were placed into one of the four transgender categories.

With regard to the qualitative data, the phone and face-to-face interviews were transcribed by the authors and then returned to the participants to make sure that their responses were presented accurately and in their own words. The e-mail and transcribed interviews were analyzed for key themes related to the research goals of understanding transgender identity formation. It is important to note that the interview method selected for this study is viewed as the least likely to lead to risks for participants and the most likely to allow access to participants' own thoughts and perspectives regarding their identity development (for examples and arguments in favor of this methodology, see, e.g., Kitzinger 1987; Lewin 1993; Weston 1997).

THE SAMPLE AND LIMITATIONS OF THE PROJECT

A total of 3,509 individuals initiated the online survey, and 3,474 respondents completed it. Given the anonymous nature of the survey and the ways in which the instrument was distributed, it is not possible to determine how many received it but chose not to participate. We do know that 35 people began the survey but did not complete it. Some of these individuals may have returned at a later time to take the survey. Others may have decided not to be involved for various reasons, including lack of time, disagreement with the approach, feeling that it was too personal or raised uncomfortable issues for them, and not having regular or consistently private online access. Respondents were given the opportunity to participate in a more detailed, follow-up interview, and interviews were arranged and conducted with 301 people by e-mail, 109 people by telephone, and 9 people face-to-face. The interviews via e-mail tended to be less in-depth than those conducted by phone or in person because e-mail limited our ability to ask follow-up questions and have interviewees expand on particular responses.

Although the results of our research demonstrate that transgender people of all ages use the Internet, our survey was limited by not being accessible to individuals who lack experience with computers or who have limited or no ability to go online. Another limitation of the study was its reliance for distribution on transgender people who had a visible presence in cyberspace. Most of the websites that offer personal profiles of transgender people are geared toward MTF individuals and female-presenting cross-dressers; these sites include URNotAlone, Susana Marques's Transgender Directory, the Vanity Club, and the Southern Belle Society. As a result, significantly more female-identified transgender individuals were contacted about and took the survey.

In addition, transgender people who are more "out," more connected to the transgender community, and more comfortable discussing their experiences were more likely to participate in the research, although some respondents did indicate that few others were aware of their current or past transgender lives. Those who offered to be interviewed were especially motivated to help educate others about their experiences, which may skew some of the results. Still, given the sample's tremendous size, our findings are likely representative of the experiences of many transgender individuals in the United States.

OVERVIEW OF CHAPTERS

In chapter 1 we review the demographics of the respondents, including gender assigned at birth, gender identity, gender expression, age, race, sexual orientation, citizenship status, physical challenges, and cognitive and/or emotional challenges. We also describe the four identity variables that will be used to examine the respondents' gendered experiences: female-to-male/transgender, male-to-female/transgender, female-to-different-gender, and male-to-different-gender. These variables are considered within the context of a discussion of the power of language within transgender communities.

The next two chapters discuss the main quantitative and qualitative findings of the survey. Chapter 2 considers how people experienced their gender identities growing up and came to identify as transgender. Some of the questions we explore are when and how people began to feel a sense of difference, to be uncertain about their gender identities, to think that they might be transgender, and to meet other transgender people. Chapter 3 addresses how the participants perceived and experienced the social climate for transgender people. We ask about safety, fear of disclosure, employment discrimination, and overt and covert harassment.

Focusing on the follow-up interviews, chapter 4 compares the experiences of individuals from different transgender groups and offers a series of "touchstones," or significant life moments, in the gender identity development processes of participants who identify as transsexual women, transsexual men, cross-dressers, and genderqueer individuals. Finally, chapter 5 discusses the specific experiences of transgender youth and the implications of these findings for institutions of higher education. We also consider how young gender-nonconforming people are changing what it means to be transgender today and what these changes will mean for future studies of transgender people.

Barbara Ann

Scout

Stephe *Zander*

I

DEMOGRAPHICS OF THE SURVEY PARTICIPANTS

> Most people have a hard time believing it at first [that I grew up
> in a female body]. They can't imagine I was ever female. . . . I
> think I live a pretty normal life. To be male is normal to me. To
> look a little different and have scars on my body is also normal
> for me.
>
> —SEAN T.

> I have always dressed as non-gender-specific as possible. I don't
> like anything too masculine or too feminine and try to hide my
> femaleness in clothing that is very straight lined and ambiguous,
> in colors that are demure [so] as to not attract undue attention
> to myself.
>
> —LINDA

"Is it a boy or a girl?" In our culture, the answer is almost always
dependent on what a physician or health care professional deter-
mines by someone's anatomy at birth. If the infant has a penis, then
it is a boy; if the infant does not, then it is a girl. Gender assignment
is thus medicalized, phallocentric, and dichotomous. The prevalence of disorders of sex development[1] aside, this binary gender
system is considered an immutable, universal fact of nature. Once
established, gender assignment evokes and prescribes boundless
sociocultural constructs. For example, the conflation of biological "sex" with the socially constructed value systems underpinning
"gender" means that people who are designated as female on the

basis of perceived anatomy are then ascribed a (subordinate) social status as girls and women (Tong 1998).

To provide a context for subsequent analysis, we begin by briefly reviewing the terminology that we will use to discuss the different aspects of gender and showing how this language offers insight into the experiences of transgender people.[2] We then present the demographics of the study respondents, including gender assigned at birth, gender identity, gender expression, sexual orientation, age, and citizenship status. We also explain the four identity variables that we have developed to describe the experiences of the respondents: female-to-male/transgender, male-to-female/transgender, female-to-different-gender, and male-to-different-gender.

THE LANGUAGE OF GENDER: TROUBLING TERMINOLOGY

If language is not correct, then what is said is not what is meant; if what is said is not what is meant, then what must be done remains undone; if this remains undone, morals and art will deteriorate; if justice goes astray, the people will stand about in helpless confusion. Hence there must be no arbitrariness in what is said. This matters above everything.

—CONFUCIUS

Language is powerful, particularly when used in "naming" people or groups of people (Fausto-Sterling 1993). The words that we use to refer to ourselves and others in terms of social characteristics (e.g., race, gender, and sexuality) reflect our own cultural values as well as those of a dominant culture (Elshtain 1998; Wood 1997).[3] Thus, how people and groups of people are named have real consequences for these individuals and their communities, as is evident in the discourses around transgender people.

Any discussion of gender difference—how people have experienced it, how the fields of science, medicine, and psychology have diagnosed and treated it, or how social activists and sociologists have responded to its medicalization—is politically charged. There are no neutral terms related to transgender people (Valentine

2007), and there are no neutral systems of classification, treatment, or strategies of empowerment. The basic point of contention pits biology against social construction; as a practical reality for transgender individuals, this means a choice between having surgery or finding acceptance and empowerment without surgery. People who do not fit the socially constructed definitions of gender are either pathologized or forced to develop a "different" sense of identity, with or without the assistance of medical intervention.

In shaping our outlook, language instills and reinforces cultural values, thereby helping to maintain social hierarchies. Julia Wood (1997) describes how language that defines and organizes our perceptions of sex and gender also furthers systems of inequality. For example, use of the generic masculine (such as using "he" to refer to both women and men or using words like "fireman," "mankind," and "man-hours") excludes and marginalizes women. As a result, men are presented as the norm while women and their experiences are viewed as deviant or unworthy of mention.

Language reinforces not only stereotypical attitudes about men and women but also dualistic notions about sex and gender. Such dichotomies are "essentialist" dead ends that scholars like philosopher Jean Elshtain suggest constitute real political dangers, since these divisions ultimately dehumanize and disempower all people (Tong 1998). For example, the common representation of women as emotional and men as rational limits the ability to recognize rationality in women and emotional expressiveness in men. Our language's emphasis on polarity (good-bad, wrong-right, male-female) also makes it difficult to think of sex, gender, gender identity, and gender expression as existing within a more dynamic framework that is inclusive of transgender people.

Although definitions facilitate discussion and the sharing of information, terminology remains subject to both cultural context and individual interpretation. As a result, the terminology that people use to describe themselves and their communities is often not universally accepted by everyone within these communities. Throughout the book, we use a number of terms and concepts with highly contested and unstable definitions. To maintain clarity, we define some of these key terms here. We also illuminate our own positions within the constantly evolving debates around the meanings of these words. Throughout the book, we use the language of the survey participants to honor their voices and their own self-descriptions. Knowing the meanings of the terms we use is important for understanding the text overall and involves going beyond the definitions themselves to how the terms relate to the lives of transgender people. Sex or biological gender is typically defined as one's biophysiological makeup. Although often reduced to genitalia, sex is established through the complex interplay between genetic, hormonal, gonadal, biochemical, and anatomical determinants that affect the physiology of the body and sexual differentiation in the brain (Caroll & Wolpe 1996; Ettner 1999; Migeon, Wisniewski, & Gearhart 2001; Money 1993; Wilson & Reiner 1999). Approximately 1.7 percent of the world's population does not fit into the biological categories—once presumed to be immutable—of female and male (Blackless et al. 2000). These individuals "do not conform to a Platonic ideal of absolute sex chromosome, gonadal, genital, and hormonal dimorphism" (161). However, they are made to fit into a gender binary, sometimes through surgery. Ruth Hubbard (1998) argues that the pressure to conform to a two-sex model has been so great in Western civilization that doctors have introduced medical interventions to "correct" sex ambiguities, thus ensuring that everyone can be easily classified as male or female.

The research is divided on who is served by these interventions—patient, parents, or medical "necessity." So-called corrective surgery for infants and children emphasizes the physical appearance of genitalia, and it is based on the idea that the appearance of people's genitals must match their gender in order for them to be considered "normal." Suzanne Kessler and Wendy McKenna (2006) argue that, in this sense, scientific knowledge does not give an answer to the question of what makes a man or a woman. Instead, "it justifies (and appears to give grounds for) the already existing knowledge that a person is either a woman or a man and that there is no problem in differentiating between the two. Biological, psychological, and social differences do not lead to our seeing two genders. Our seeing two genders leads to the 'discovery' of biological, psychological, and social differences" (178). Other authors (e.g., Greenberg

2006) argue that "sex" is not completely determined by biology and that "gender" is not completely determined by processes of social construction. The aforementioned divisions disrupt deeply ingrained notions about sex and gender in our society. Indeed, both the prevalence of individuals with disorders of sex development (DSD) and their negative responses to unnecessary surgical interventions challenge the fundamental assumption that physical characteristics unequivocally define male and female. The experiences of people with DSD demonstrate how sex is socially and, at times, physically constructed.

One of the individuals we interviewed for our study, Burton, thinks that he was possibly born with an intersex condition but is uncertain what surgeries he might have been subjected to as an infant. From his earliest memories, he gravitated toward maleness and did not accept being seen as female. He "didn't feel it was right." Over time, however, Burton gave in to social pressure to identify as female, believing that he had no other social option. Not until he met another transgender man did he realize that he was not bound by the biological dichotomy imposed on him.

Similar to biological sex, *gender* has traditionally been considered a dichotomous social construction: one is either a man or a woman (Butler 1990; Feinberg 1998; Wilchins 2002). The distinction between gender and sex, as described by anthropologist Gayle Rubin (1975), is that gender is the "socially imposed division of the sexes that transforms males and females into 'men' and 'women'" (40). A substantial body of literature (Butler 1990; Cameron 2005; Gagné et al. 1997; Vertinsky 1990; Wilchins 2002) suggests that physical differences between women and men are used to rationalize distinctions in expectations and opportunities based on gender. Despite shifting cultural practices during the twentieth century and changing notions about what is considered to be gender-appropriate behavior, a binary model of women and men—of femaleness and maleness—remains intact. Physical differences that do not align with gender expectations are categorized as abnormal, and identities that do not align are pathologized as undesirable but treatable mental disorders (Butler 2004). A lack of openness to difference and a general uneasiness with gender difference further reinforce a belief in two separate and distinct genders. Society does not offer any social or biological territory for individuals who exist between sexes and genders. According to Hubbard (1998), physical and behavior modification became the solution to sustain congruency between sex and gender.

Gender involves not only *gender assignment*—the gender label given to someone at birth based on their perceived sex—but also gender attribution, gender roles, gender identity, and gender expression (Bornstein 1994). *Gender attribution* is how others perceive one's gender. It is based on an individual's appearance and also on the *gender roles*—the behaviors that are culturally coded as masculine or feminine—that someone assumes. Gender attribution and gender roles may or may not coincide with each other and with one's birth gender. For example, Debra, a sixty-two-year-old white participant who describes herself as "a cross-dresser with a little drag queen thrown in for good measure," is over six feet tall before she "don[s] a Texas wig and platform heels." So even when she cross-dresses and takes on traditionally female gender roles, she is still typically perceived as having been assigned male at birth. Debra admits that her appearance "makes it kind of difficult to skulk about without being noticed," but that is the point: she takes pride in her gender identity and refuses to be invisible.

Gender identity refers to an individual's sense of hir own gender, which may be different from one's birth gender or how others perceive one's gender. The centering of gender on an individual's self-concept, instead of on the person's biological sex, creates a discursive space that allows for a more nuanced understanding of gender. The complex ways that people understand their gender is reflected in the experiences of many of the study participants. For example, Reid, a white forty-seven-year-old respondent, recognizes that he is not "female" yet also feels that "male" is not quite accurate, either: "I had an epiphany, realizing I had not transitioned from female-to-male, but from female-to-not-female. What 'not-female' means to me is that I would have ended up happily male if I'd been born and raised male, but since I was raised female, that has affected my world view and brain development such that I cannot be the man I would have been otherwise."

Gender expression refers to how one chooses to indicate one's gender identity to others through behavior and appearance, which includes clothing, hairstyle, makeup, voice, and body characteristics. Gender expression can vary over time and in different contexts, as demonstrated by individuals who cross-dress on a limited basis or who do so only when circumstances permit. Julie, a white thirty-three-year-old cross-dresser, "spends as much time in a female role as possible," but her life does not always allow it. In particular, Julie's father is against her cross-dressing, and they work for the same company—a place where her father has worked for thirty-five years. Having to hide her identity at work is "a big sticking point in [her] life." Julie has learned to balance how she presents, switching back and forth to respect boundaries. She often expresses her gender as male in public as a "convenience issue," but on most weekends she is her female self.

Genderism refers to the beliefs and practices that privilege stable, binary gender identities/expressions and that subordinate and disparage transgender people and other individuals who do not adhere to dominant gender expectations (Wilchins 2002). The term encompasses individual acts of discrimination as well as systemic and institutionalized inequalities, such as insurance coverage that excludes medical care related to gender transitioning and public bathrooms that are limited to "men" and "women." Genderism is also evident in the binary basis of much of the language involving gender—from the ways in which women and men are conceptualized, to the lack of acceptance for gender-neutral pronouns, to the common use of gendered forms of address such as "sir" and "ma'am."

THE SEX, GENDER IDENTITY, AND GENDER EXPRESSION
OF THE RESPONDENTS

As noted previously, the online survey that formed the basis for this book was open to all who identified in some way as "transgender," whether or not they used this particular label for themselves and whether or not they still considered themselves to be transgender.

To be inclusive of all gender-nonconforming people, we defined "transgender" broadly as "anyone who transgresses or blurs traditional gender categories." We also sought to reach a wide variety of transgender people in publicizing and recruiting for the survey by contacting transgender groups and individuals in all fifty states and the District of Columbia. A total of 3,474 respondents completed the survey. The following sections provide a summary of the responses to the demographic questions in the survey, which will serve as a foundation for the analyses and reviews provided in subsequent chapters.

Sex. The respondents were asked the sex assigned to them at birth. More than three-fourths of the participants (2,648 people) were assigned male at birth, and less than one-fourth (807 people) were assigned female. Nineteen participants (0.5 percent) chose not to identify their assigned sex (see table 1.1).

The overrepresentation of respondents who were considered male at birth was a result, we feel, of transsexual women and female-presenting cross-dressers being generally more visible on the Web and more involved in organized support groups than are transgender men. The former were thus more likely to encounter and participate in the survey. This limitation is substantiated by a recent study (NGLTF/NCTE 2009) that examined discrimination among transgender people. In that study, 60 percent of the sample identified the sex on their birth certificate as male and 40 percent as female.

Gender Identity. Gender constitutes one of the most important, salient, and pervasive social categories (Maass, Cadinu, Guarnieri,

TABLE 1.1   Gender assigned at birth

Gender Assigned	%	n
Female	23.2	807
Male	76.2	2,648
Missing data	0.5	19

& Grasselli 2003). The participants were given the option of identifying their gender identity as female, male, transgender, or another identity. Within the "transgender" and the "other" identity response choices, respondents were offered the option of specifying how they currently choose to identify. Among the people assigned female at birth, 45 percent refer to themselves today as male, 36 percent as transgender, and 13 percent as "other." Almost half of the people assigned male at birth now describe themselves as female, 35 percent as transgender, and 6 percent as "other." Six percent of the female-assigned and 12 percent of the male-assigned individuals continue to identify with their birth gender. However, they still consider themselves to be transgender because they cross-dress, present part-time as a different gender, or otherwise challenge gender norms.

The participants who described their gender identity as "transgender" and "other" were asked to elaborate, and they referred to themselves using a wide variety of terms. The 1,211 individuals who identified specifically as "transgender" provided 502 additional descriptors for their gender identities, of which 479 were unique responses. The other 23 responses, each of which was given by at least two participants, are shown in table 1.2. The most common descriptors were "cross-dresser" (256 people), "male to female" (246), "female to male" (98), and "genderqueer" (59). Of the 257 "other" responses, the most common descriptors were "genderqueer" (41 people), "cross-dresser" (29 people), and "androgynous/androgyne" (18 people).

The responses in table 1.2 are provided by age in order to explore trends in language related to gender identity across the life span. Most of the "transgender" respondents who further described their gender identities as "male to female," "cross-dresser," "a combination of both [male and female]," "transvestite/transsexual," or "non-op" were at least thirty-three years old. Donna, for example, indicated that she grew up at a time before there was a name for how she felt: "Transgender, genderqueer . . . these terms didn't exist—at least not as we know them now. There were no resources—like the Internet—which I could consult to help me cope with how I felt. I was very much alone with my 'dark secrets' and it was not until I went online in 1997 that I realized how un-alone I was."

TABLE I.2A   Transgender responses by age (*n* = 1,211)

Specific Transgender Identity	18 and Under (*n*)	19–22 (*n*)	23–32 (*n*)	33–42 (*n*)	43–52 (*n*)	53 and Over (*n*)	Total (*n*)
Male to female	7	17	39	62	48	73	246
Cross-dresser	1	10	23	59	82	81	256
Female to male	21	36	27	11		3	98
Genderqueer	22	31	6				59
Transvestite/ Transsexual		3	8	12	21	11	55
Post-op F2M (2); M2F (31); No gender (2)	2	3	2	8	2	18	35
Trannyboy/ Transguy/Man	3	12	6	3		1	25
Androgynous/ Androgyne	2	5	4	2	7	8	28
Non-op F2M (5); M2F (15); TS (7); Transmale (1)		2	3	4	12	7	28
A combination of both	3		1	4	17	6	31
Pre-op F2M (2); M2F (1); No gender (1)		2	2	3	1	2	10
Transwoman		1	2	1		3	7
Bigender					5	6	11
Intersex		1	2	2			5
Shemale	1	1	1		2	2	7
Transgendered	1		2	1	9	1	14
Two-spirit			2	2	2	1	7
Mostly female			1	2	10	1	15
Part-time		1	1	2			4
50% male, 50% female						3	3
60% male, 40% female						3	3
Butch		2					2
I am my own gender					2	2	4
Other responses							479

TABLE I.2B   "Other" gender identity responses (*n* = 257)

Other Responses	Totals (*n*)
Genderqueer	41
Cross-dresser	29
Androgynous/Androgyne	18
Unsure/Don't know	11
Bigender	9
Both female and male	8
Queer	6
Questioning	5
Transsexual	5
Intersex	4
Confused	3
Neutral	3
Two-spirited	3
Un-gendered	3
Intergender	2
Shemale	2
Transvestite	2
Transman	2
Other responses	101

In contrast, most of the "transgender" respondents who also characterized themselves as "female to male," "genderqueer," and "trannyboy/transguy/man" were younger than thirty-three years old. Masen, an FTM interviewee, met and became friends with a very butch dyke, whom he saw as similarly gendered. The friend subsequently transitioned, which Masen was "fascinated by." He never imagined it was possible—it was "like going to the moon." Masen moved to San Francisco in 1995, where he met other trans people and began to question the stereotypes and assumptions he had about transgender people. Instead of "the *Jerry Springer* version," he met sane people who had jobs and were happy with their lives.

When asked to elaborate on their gender identities, the 257 participants who characterized themselves as "other" (rather than female, male, or transgender) used 119 additional descriptors for themselves, of which 101 were unique responses. The most common responses were "genderqueer" (41 people), "cross-dresser"

(29), "androgynous/androgyne" (18), "bigender" or "both female and male" (17), and "unsure/don't know" (11). These results also are reported in table 1.2. Thus, the participants who described their gender identities as "other" used some of the same descriptors in naming their identities as did the "transgender" participants, reflecting the fact that even people who use a common terminology can have a very different understanding of what those words mean. One of the participants, Sam, recently began to identify as genderqueer. Sam tells people that ze is an FTM when it would be easier for them to understand. But ze does not identify as an FTM because ze has "an androgynous personality emotionally." Sam also does not want "to deny or change certain parts of [hir]self." Ze feels that ze is "between two genders."

Another participant, Caiden, identifies as transgender or as a transfag. His gender expression is "somewhere in the middle." He is not male-identified but not female either. He is perceived differently at different times. On hir twenty-eighth birthday, 'Ron began to identify as genderqueer. For 'Ron, genderqueer means that hir gender is not determined by hir reproductive organs; in hir day-to-day life, ze embodies different aspects assigned to different genders.

Although the respondents who indicated an "other" gender identity saw their experiences as part of the larger category "transgender" (hence their willingness to participate in a survey on transgender identity), some chose not to refer to themselves as transgender because they identified in nonbinary ways and saw "transgender" (which literally means "across gender") as more applicable to people who were transitioning from one gender to another. Esther, for example, identified hir gender identity on the survey as "other" and specified that ze is genderqueer. Ze went on to explain: "Until I learned about the 'genderqueer' term, I'd never met anyone else like me. I'd met transgendered people and trans-sexuals, but it's not the same."

The participants who described themselves as transgender and the participants who did not identify as male, female, or transgender often viewed their identities very differently; however, there was not a clear distinction between the participants who indicated that their gender identity was male or female and the male or female transgender participants, respectively. For example, whereas some MTF respondents reported that their gender identity was female, other MTF respondents stated that they were transgender and explained that they identified as female. Given the lack of significant differences between the male/female and transgender identity categories, we combined the groups to create two new variables: female-to-male/transgender (FTM/T, n = 653) and male-to-female/transgender (MTF/T, n = 2,178).

To describe the myriad ways that those who transgress choose to gender identify, we also created the shorthand term "different gender" to refer to participants who did not choose "man" or "woman" as their gender identification. For example, some of the individuals surveyed who were designated female at birth did not feel that this gender assignment fit them, but they did not identify as male either. One such participant, "Kody," is taking testosterone and has had chest surgery as part of his process of transitioning from a female-looking to a more male-looking appearance. But despite being seen by others as a man, he does not identify as male. Instead, Kody considers himself to have had a "multi-gendered life" that does not conform to a gender binary. The female-assigned participants who identified and referred to themselves in various ways besides male and female—such as "transgender," "genderqueer," "trannyboy," "transmen," and "transguy"—were grouped together for the purposes of our analysis into the category female-to-different-gender (FTDG, n = 104). The individuals assigned male at birth who identified not as male or female but rather as "transwomen," "transgendered girl," "tranny girl," and the like were similarly combined into the category male-to-different-gender (MTDG, n = 152).

Gender Expression. We also asked the respondents to identify their current gender expression. The response choices were "feminine," "masculine," "transgender," or "other." Overall, 40 percent present as female, 26 percent as male, and 25 percent as transgender. Nine percent characterize their gender expression as "other." Among the ways that this last group express their gender identities are through presenting as "ambiguous," "androgynous,"

TABLE 1.3   Gender identity by gender expression

	Gender Identity			
	Woman	Man	Transgender	Other
Gender Expression	% (*n*)	% (*n*)	% (*n*)	% (n)
Female/Feminine	72.4 (950)	13.4 (90)	23.8 (288)	19.1 (49)
Male/Masculine	10.2 (134)	64.9 (437)	21.6 (262)	21.0 (54)
Transgender	12.2 (160)	14.7 (99)	47.1 (570)	7.4 (19)
Other	4.8 (63)	6.2 (42)	7.0 (85)	51.8 (133)
Missing data	< 1 (6)	< 1 (5)	< 1 (6)	< 1 (2)

"bigender," "both female and male," "butch," "cross-dresser," "fluid," "genderqueer," and "varies." For example, "Mar" calls himself "bigendered." "I don't identify as a woman or a man but as me," she states. "I enjoy living both as a man and a woman. Each unique gender gives me different outlets in which to express my person and interact with others. I find such a lifestyle both enjoyable and fulfilling, giving me access to experiences and relationships that just are not open to mono-gendered individuals."

Approximately three-quarters of the female-identified respondents described their gender expression today as female, and two-thirds of the male-identified respondents described their gender expression today as male. Almost half of the transgender-identified participants expressed themselves as transgender. The remainder of the transgender people were about evenly divided between individuals who present as female and those who present as male (table 1.3).

OTHER SELECTED CHARACTERISTICS OF THE RESPONDENTS

The respondents were asked to provide demographic information in addition to sex assigned at birth, gender identity, and gender expression. Although the focus of this book is on transgender identity, the following characteristics are considered here in order to provide a more detailed profile of the participants in the project.

Age. We offered the respondents six age categories to choose from: eighteen and under, nineteen to twenty-two, twenty-three to thirty-two, thirty-three to forty-two, forty-three to fifty-two, and fifty-three and over. These particular age categories were created so that we could focus on the experiences of traditionally college-aged transgender people (nineteen- to twenty-two-year-olds). There were a significant number of respondents in each age group, which allows us to consider the experiences of transgender people across the life span. Approximately 70 percent of the participants (2,379 people) were between twenty-three and fifty-two years old. Even though only 10 percent of the respondents were younger than nineteen and only 5 percent were older than fifty-two, these two age groups had substantial numbers of participants (330 and 173, respectively) because of the large sample size.

When reviewing the data in terms of our gender identity variables (FTM/T, MTF/T, FTDG, and MTDG), more than half (57 percent) of the respondents who were assigned female at birth and who now identify as male or transgender (i.e., FTM/T) are less than twenty-two years old; of the respondents who were assigned male at birth and who now identify as female or transgender (i.e., MTF/T), more than half (59 percent) are between thirty-three and fifty-two years old. The majority of the participants (72 percent) who were assigned female at birth and who now identify their gender as other than female, male, or transgender (i.e., FTDG) are less than twenty-two years old, whereas most respondents (76 percent) who were assigned male at birth and who now identify as having a different gender (i.e., MTDG) are between twenty-three and fifty-two years old. Overall, then, the individuals in the study who were assigned male at birth and who identify today as female, transgender, or a different gender were substantially *older* than the individuals who were assigned female at birth. This age difference is an important factor in subsequent analysis.

For example, one area in which the age of the participants was significant is in the availability of information about transgender people. "Jessica," a sixty-four-year-old cross-dressing interviewee, offered that she saw almost nothing about her experiences when growing up in the 1940s and 1950s. She remembers coming across a story about Christine Jorgensen, which she reread a number of times because it "tweaked [her] interest greatly." Years later, Jessica found a copy of *Transgender Tapestry* in an adult bookstore, through which she learned about a gender therapist in her area. In contrast, when Airen, a thirty-one-year-old FTM interviewee, went to college in the 1990s, even nontransgender students were cognizant of transgender people. They pointed out—"not necessarily maliciously"—the ways in which they did not see him as fitting in as a woman or as a dyke. Some of these experiences and conversations led Airen "to question whether [he] actually *did* feel associated with [his] assigned gender of female and assumed gender identity of girl, woman, et cetera and about the ways in which [he] was uncomfortable in [his] body."

Race. We provided participants with the opportunity to mark multiple boxes regarding their racial identity, allowing them to identify as biracial or multiracial. Eighty-seven percent of the respondents (3,007 people) indicated that they are white or European American, and 12 percent (422 people) indicated that they are a person of color.[4] Among the individuals surveyed who identified as people of color, the largest group was American Indians (152 people). They were followed by people who identified as Latino(a)/Hispanic/Chicano(a) (128 people), Asian/Asian American (87), African/African American/black (78), Middle Eastern (30), Pacific Islander (10), Hawaiian Native (7), and Alaskan Native (5). These findings are consistent with the NGLTF/NCTE (2009) survey on the prevalence of discrimination against transgender people, in which the majority of the sample was white (84 percent) and the largest group of people of color was American Indian (6 percent).

A summary of the respondents' race by gender identity is provided in table 1.4. Within each racial group, the majority of respondents identified as male-to-female/transgender.

Sexual Orientation. The American Psychological Association (2010) states that sexual orientation is "an enduring emotional, romantic, sexual, or affectional attraction toward others." Sexual orientation also refers to a person's sense of identity based on these

TABLE I.4   Race/ethnicity by FTDG, FTM/T, MTDG, MTF/T

				Gender Identity				
	FTDG		FTM/T		MTDG		MTF/T	
Racial Identity	*n*	%	*n*	%	*n*	%	*n*	%
African/African American/black (*n* = 67)	6	8.9	25	37.3	2	2.9	34	50.7
American Indian (*n* = 145)	9	6.2	32	22.1	8	5.5	96	66.2
Alaska Native (*n* = 5)	1	20.0	1	20.0	0	0.0	3	60.0
Asian/Asian American (*n* = 80)	3	3.7	15	18.8	4	5.0	58	72.5
Latino(a)/Hispanic/ Chicano(a) (*n* = 113)	7	6.1	35	30.9	6	5.3	65	57.5
Middle Eastern (*n* = 26)	2	7.6	8	30.8	1	3.8	15	57.6
Pacific Islander (*n* = 10)	1	10.0	1	10.0	1	10.0	7	70.0
Hawaiian Native (*n* = 7)	0	0.0	2	28.5	1	14.3	4	57.1
White/Caucasian (*n* = 2,849)	95	3.3	592	20.7	144	5.7	2,018	70.8

Note: Because some respondents did not indicate their gender identity, the *n* for each racial identity may be less than the sample's total number of respondents for that racial category.

attractions and subsequent behavior as well as membership in a community of others who share one's attractions. Since the work of Alfred Kinsey in the 1940s and 1950s, research has demonstrated that sexual orientation ranges along a continuum from exclusive attraction to members of a different sex to exclusive attraction to members of the same sex. However, sexual orientation is usually discussed more narrowly in terms of three distinct, immutable categories: heterosexual, gay/lesbian, and bisexual.

The view that sexual orientation is fixed and unalterable has been challenged from a variety of theoretical perspectives, including labeling theory, life span development theory, social constructionism, and evolutionary psychology (see, e.g., Baumeister 2000; D'Augelli 1994b; Diamond & Savin-Williams 2003; Kitzinger &

Wilkinson 1995; Richardson 1984). Theorists in these areas suggest that sexual orientation is inherently flexible and that it develops continuously over the life span out of an individual's sexual and emotional experiences, social interactions, and cultural influences. From this standpoint, individuals may experience transitions in sexual orientation throughout their lives.

Note also that a person's self-described sexual orientation may not always correspond to that person's sexual attractions. For example, some transsexual people indicate that they are more attracted to different-sex individuals post-transition but remain committed to the same-sex partners they had before transitioning, or vice versa (Samons 2009). In addition, some transgender people of color who are attracted to others of the same sex do not identify themselves as "lesbian," "gay," or "bisexual," viewing these terms as white social constructs. Instead, they may describe themselves as "same-gender loving" and, in some cases, as "heterosexual," or they might not attach a label to their sexual orientation (Battle, Cohen, Fergerson, & Audam 2002; Rankin 2003). Because of these complexities, we requested that the respondents characterize both their sexual orientation and their sexual attractions. For sexual orientation, the participants could state that they were asexual, bisexual, gay, lesbian, heterosexual, or another identity. In terms of sexual attraction, respondents were asked to indicate whether they were most sexually attracted to women, men, both men and women, or were uncertain.

Because sexual orientation is tied to one's gender and the gender of one's partner(s), transgender people—especially individuals with nonbinary gender identities—often face a unique challenge in attaching a label to their sexual identity. For example, if someone does not identify as male or female, how does that person refer to hir sexual orientation? How does a female-presenting cross-dresser who is attracted to men while cross-dressed, but to women when not in "women's" clothing, identify hirself?

Even transgender people who fully transition and who see themselves (and are seen by others) as male or female may still struggle with how to name their sexual orientation. In particular, some of the FTM/transgender and female-to-different-gender participants who were attracted to women and who had their roots in the lesbian community continued to identify as "lesbian," "queer," "a dyke," or "nonstraight"—even though they no longer considered themselves female—because they did not want to erase their pasts and did not feel that the label "heterosexual" adequately reflected their experiences. Eric, for example, stated, "I used to identify as a dyke very strongly and still do, just in a different way. I was occupying a more female space, but now a more masculine space, but not really as male." Another participant, Michael W., also sought to remain connected to his pretransition sexual identity:

I lived openly as a dyke for more than 20 years and no number of shots [of testosterone] . . . will ever change my history. Nor do I have any interest in that happening . . . . I've been without my lesbian ID card for several years now, but I can't really call myself straight either. I really have no concept of "straight" as a life experience . . . so "heteroqueer" seems to fit best, or "I'm a guy who likes girls who like 'special' guys."

Almost one-third of the study respondents (1,120 people) reported that their sexual orientation was bisexual, and 30 percent (1,029 people) identified as heterosexual. Sixteen percent (567 people) marked "other." Among the ways that members of this latter group described their sexual orientation were "a mix of asexual, gay, and heterosexual," "ambivalent," "attracted to genderqueer people," "autobisexual," "bisexual when dressed in female clothes otherwise heterosexual," "pansexual," "queer," and "transgender lesbian."

A review of the respondents' sexual orientation by their gender identity shows that slightly more than one-third of the FTM/T participants characterized their sexual orientation as "other," 28 percent identified as heterosexual, and 20 percent identified as bisexual (table 1.5).

The majority of these "other" respondents described themselves as queer or pansexual. Fifty-one percent of the female-to-different-gender participants also indicated "other" as their sexual orientation. Like the FTM/T respondents, the majority identified

TABLE 1.5   Gender identity by sexual orientation

Sexual Orientation	Gender Identity							
	FTM/T		FTDG		MTF/T		MTDG	
	%	n	%	n	%	n	%	n
Asexual	2.1	14	5.8	6	6.3	137	3.9	6
Bisexual	20.4	133	15.4	16	36.2	789	38.2	58
Gay	10.4	68	5.8	6	1.7	36	5.3	8
Lesbian	4.4	29	16.3	17	15.9	347	6.6	10
Heterosexual	27.7	181	5.8	6	29.2	637	24.3	37
Other	34.5	225	51.0	53	10.3	224	21.7	33
Missing data	0.5	3	0.0	0	0.4	8	0.0	0

as either queer or pansexual. Among MTF/transgender and male-to-different-gender respondents, the predominant sexual orientations were bisexual (respectively 36 percent and 38 percent) and heterosexual (respectively 29 percent and 24 percent). Twenty-two percent of the MTDG participants indicated that their sexual orientation was "other." Again, most of the individuals who chose "other" stated that their sexual orientation was either queer or pansexual.

Examining the data by sexual orientation and gender expression reveals that 37 percent of the participants who expressed themselves as female/feminine described their sexual orientation as bisexual, 26 percent identified themselves as heterosexual, and 19 percent as lesbian. Thirty-eight percent of the respondents who expressed themselves as male/masculine described their sexual orientation as heterosexual, and 28 percent identified as bisexual. The respondents who presented as transgender were equally split between bisexual and heterosexual individuals—about one-third identified as each. In addition, the participants who expressed themselves as female/feminine were more likely than the participants who expressed themselves as male/masculine or as transgender to characterize themselves as asexual.

Not surprisingly, the vast majority (87 percent) of the FTM/T respondents who identified as gay indicated that they were primarily attracted to men, and the vast majority (92 percent) of the FTM/T respondents who identified as heterosexual indicated that they were primarily attracted to women. Similarly, the MTF/T participants who described themselves as lesbians overwhelmingly reported that they were primarily attracted to women (93 percent). However, only 33 percent of the MTF/T participants who reported that they were heterosexual were primarily attracted to men. Many more (55 percent) were primarily attracted to women, perhaps because they maintained their marriages to women after they transitioned. Among the FTM/T and MTF/T participants who characterized themselves as bisexual, fewer than half (respectively 47 percent and 44 percent) indicated that their attraction was primarily to both women and men; the majority were attracted more to women or more to men. Another noteworthy finding was that a small number (28) of the FTM/T respondents self-identified as lesbians, despite not identifying as female, and were primarily attracted to women. Likewise, a small number (31) of the MTF/T respondents described themselves as gay, despite not identifying as male, and were primarily attracted to men.

Physical/Emotional/Cognitive Challenges. Eleven percent of the respondents in our project offered that they had some form of physical disability. These disabilities ranged from degenerative diseases, such as arthritis and cardiorespiratory concerns, to hearing and seeing limitations. The prevalence of these conditions in the transgender population appears to be no greater than in the cisgender population. However, research by Shannon Chavez Korell and Peggy Lorah (2007) does suggest that, as a group, transgender people are more likely than cisgender people to experience mood disorders, anxiety disorders, low self-esteem, and depression. The authors suggest that these cognitive/emotional challenges result from a lack of adequate support systems, family issues or the impact of transgender identity on families, social and emotional stressors from the pervasive pattern of discrimination and prejudice experienced by transgender people, and their general lack of social acceptance.

In our study, 22 percent of the respondents stated that they had a cognitive or emotional attribute that substantially affects a major life activity. Of these 771 participants, 71 percent reported that the attribute was mild, moderate, or severe depression (16 percent of all participants). Care must be taken when interpreting these results, however, because the responses are self-reports and not clinical diagnoses. For many participants, depression resulted from not being able to live as the gender they felt themselves to be. Ted, an FTM interviewee, became depressed and felt suicidal when his body began developing in ways he did not want. Similarly, MTF interviewee Leslie prayed in grade school that she would have a body that matched her female mind. She became depressed when she could not resolve the difference between the two. Another MTF participant, Allason, experienced anxiety and depression problems when having to act male, but she was forced to wear what she calls "a male mask in order to conform to the pressures of society."

Subsequent chapters will draw on the demographic characteristics of the respondents outlined in this chapter. In particular, the findings will be analyzed with regard to the participants' identities of FTM/transgender, female-to-different-gender, MTF/transgender, and male-to-different-gender. In chapter 2, we examine how people experienced their gender identity growing up and how they came to identify as transgender. Some of the questions that we explore concern when and how the participants began to feel a sense of gender difference, when they began to feel uncertain about their gender identity, when they thought that they might be transgender, and when and how they began to meet other transgender people.

Charlene

Nora and her wife, Lolita, and daughter, Lara

Ted

Turner

2

EXPERIENCES OF TRANSGENDER IDENTITY

Since I was a child, I realized I could not express my feelings, and forced myself to present myself as a male. It is one of the loneliest decisions a child could ever make. No one can know you.

—JERI

Whether transgender people identify as female-to-male (FTM) or male-to-female (MTF) transsexual individuals, cross-dressers, genderqueers, androgynes, or as other nonbinary gender identities, they feel different from others of their assigned gender and question the social expectations that result from this gender assignment. The time in their lives when transgender individuals recognize themselves as "different" varies, as do how they experience and feel about their sense of difference. Uncertainty about their gender identity leads some people to search for information about what they are experiencing and to claim a transgender identity readily. Others repress their feelings and acknowledge themselves as transgender only when they reach a time in their lives when they can no longer remain in denial. For some, learning about or meeting other transgender people serves as a catalyst for self-recognition and acceptance, as they see themselves in others and realize that they are not alone in how they feel.

In this chapter, we examine how people experienced their gender identity growing up and how they came to identify as transgender. Some of the questions we consider are when and how the participants began to feel a sense of gender difference, when they began to feel uncertain about their gender identity, when they thought that they might be transgender, when and how they began to meet other transgender people, and what they experienced when they came out to partners, children, and parents. We will pay particular attention to how the participants' responses often varied by age and gender identity, since these were the most salient differences.

A SENSE OF BEING "DIFFERENT"

The survey requested respondents to identify when they began to feel "different" from others because of how they perceived their gender. The vast majority of members of all four of the study's gender identity categories—86 percent of female-to-male/transgender (FTM/T) individuals, 86 percent of male-to-female/transgender (MTF/T) individuals, 80 percent of male-to-different-gender (MTDG) individuals, and 70 percent of female-to-different-gender (FTDG) individuals—indicated that they felt unlike others at or before the age of twelve. Reviewing the results by the age of the participants when they took the survey, most people in each of the study's age brackets (eighteen and under, nineteen to twenty-two, twenty-three to thirty-two, thirty-three to forty-two, forty-three to fifty-two, and fifty-three and over) also felt different before their teen years. The individuals surveyed who were eighteen and younger and those who were fifty-three and older were somewhat less likely than the other participants (73 percent and 76 percent, respectively, versus 81–88 percent) to have considered themselves to be different before they turned thirteen years old. But more than 90 percent of members of all age groups realized that they did not fit in with others of their assigned gender by the end of their teen years.

A sense of gender difference often occurred very early in childhood, when the respondents first realized that distinctions were made between girls and boys. In the follow-up telephone and face-to-face interviews, the participants were asked to specify when they began to recognize themselves as different from other people of their assigned gender. Rhiannon, a forty-eight-year-old transsexual woman of American Indian (Cree, Anashinabe, Assinboine, and Metis) and Celtic ancestry, "knew something was different, but didn't know what it was" when she was four or five years old. She occasionally cross-dressed wearing her mother's clothes, and remembers once putting on her mother's bikini and showing her. From her mother's negative response and other hostile reactions, Rhiannon learned to keep her gender identity to herself and repressed her sense of herself as female until her mid-twenties.

Mark, a forty-one-year-old Cuban American transsexual man, also encountered family opposition to his gender expression. Since the age of three or four, Mark "felt different." He did not enjoy playing with dolls or traditionally female toys and would only wear dresses when forced to do so by his mother. The more he rebelled as a child, the more his family tried to make him act feminine, fearing that he would become a lesbian woman. Another FTM participant, Turner, likewise rejected traditionally feminine roles from a young age. Seeing himself as a boy "from as far back as [he] can remember," Turner could not understand why others treated him as a girl. One memory that particularly stands out for him was being dressed as Minnie Mouse, rather than Mickey, for a tap dance recital when he was three or four years old. Turner was hurt and confused, as it "was not who [he] was."

Twenty-three (19 percent) of the participants interviewed by telephone or in person said that they "always" or from their "earliest memories" felt a sense of gender dissonance. For example, "Carol," a white fifty-nine-year-old woman who was assigned male at birth, states that there was "never a time" when she did not feel that "something was wrong" with her for not identifying as her birth gender. When she was young, she would play fantasy games with other children in which she could be female. But Carol was often unable to persuade others to treat her as a girl and was frequently beaten up by other children for liking feminine things. As a result, she learned to hide herself, so that no one except her wife knew that she identified as female until she was in her forties.

Of the seventy-five phone interviewees who provided an esti-mated age for when they began to recognize themselves as different from others of their assigned gender, the mean age was 5.4 years old. This finding is in line with the results of the groundbreaking research of Lawrence Kohlberg (1966), who suggests that children develop a sense of gender consistency, a belief that their gender will not change, between the ages of five and seven. Before then, ac-cording to Kohlberg, children fail to understand that people cannot change genders the way that they might change clothing or jobs. Obviously, transgender children are unlikely to achieve a sense of constancy in the gender assigned to them at birth. Even so, by about age seven they begin to recognize that their identities are incongruent with their gender assignment and that this difference sets them apart from other children. In the current survey, a num-ber of the interviewees—who, as young children, prayed before they went to sleep at night that they would wake up a different gender—realized by age six or seven that this wish would not come true. They were not going to change into the boy or girl that they felt themselves to be.

Other research also shows that many transgender people realize that they are gender different at a young age. In her study of ninety-seven MTF transgender clients, social worker Sandra Samons (2009) finds that the women were first aware of being transgender from their earliest memories to age fourteen, with a median age of five years old. Similarly, among the eleven transsexual women inter-viewed by Anne Bolin (1988), the modal age at which they began to recognize themselves as female was five years old. Many reported that they started to cross-dress around this age or shortly thereafter. The fifty-five FTM and MTF transgender youths studied by Gross-man, D'Augelli, Howell, and Hubbard (2005) felt "different from others" at a mean age of 7.5 years. The age at which they felt this sense of difference ranged from three to twelve years old for the FTM participants and one to fourteen years old for the MTF par-ticipants, with most indicating that they always wished to be born and to wear the clothing "of the sex other than their birth sex" (9). In addition, two-thirds of both groups reported that other people told them that they were "different from others" in early childhood.

Many female-presenting cross-dressers likewise felt a sense of gender difference and began to cross-dress in early childhood. The mean age at which a sample of 372 cross-dressers surveyed by Bonnie and Vern Bullough (1997) started to cross-dress was 8.5 years old, with slightly more than one-third indicating that they first experienced cross-dressing by age six and more than 90 percent by age fourteen. Other studies have reached similar conclusions. For example, Richard Docter and Virginia Prince (1997) find that two-thirds of the more than 1,000 cross-dressers in their sample initially cross-dressed prior to age ten and 95 percent did so by age twenty, and Gagné et al. (1997) find that about three-fourths of the seventeen cross-dressers they interviewed began cross-dressing in childhood; the rest started during adolescence.

HOW PARTICIPANTS EXPERIENCED BEING
GENDER DIFFERENT

Almost all of the people (97 percent) who responded to our survey indicated that they recognized themselves as being different from others of their assigned gender by the end of the teenage years. But how they experienced this sense of difference varied widely. The individuals who were assigned female at birth and who now identify as men, transgender, or another gender were much more likely than the male-assigned individuals who now identify as women, transgender, or another gender to have had a negative emotional reaction when they became aware of their gender difference. The contrast was especially pronounced between the female-to-different-gender (FTDG) and male-to-different-gender (MTDG) respondents, with the FTDG participants feeling more angry (36 versus 17 percent), more marginalized (51 versus 30 percent), and more suicidal (35 versus 13 percent) than the MTDG participants. At the same time, however, the FTDG respondents were generally less fearful (42 versus 54 percent) and more comfortable (22 versus 13 percent) with their gender identity.

A number of the FTM interviewees shared moving stories about how they felt when they recognized themselves as gender different.

Andre—who, as a young child, went to bed each night hoping to wake up as a boy—remembers having a nightmare in which his siblings rolled a boulder on him and buried him alive. Being forced to bury his gender identity underneath a "little girl shell" was like that nightmare to him, and he had "waves of feeling suicidal" during his childhood. Another FTM participant, Ryan, attempted suicide twice while in college because he could not cope with the discordance between how his body looked and how he felt about himself. Perhaps because he subconsciously wanted a less female-looking body, he also experienced anorexia at the same time. Ryan eventually came across the concept of "transgender" when he was in graduate school, which helped him to begin to understand and accept himself.

The contrast in reactions upon realizing that they were gender different may be explained by the younger mean ages of the FTM/transgender and female-to-different-gender respondents (65 percent of whom were less than twenty-three years old) as compared with the mean ages of the MTF/transgender and male-to-different-gender respondents (only 17 percent of whom were less than twenty-three). The individuals who were twenty-two years old or younger at the time of the study were more likely than the older individuals to feel marginalized, angry, and suicidal when they first felt different from others of their assigned gender. The younger participants also felt more fearful, but the disparity between the younger and the older participants was less than for the other negative emotional reactions. For people of all ages, other common reactions to feeling gender different included confusion, shame, isolation/loneliness, and depression.

A common perception is that young transgender people today have it easier than transgender people in past decades because of the greater availability of resources and support services. However, our findings demonstrate that many transgender youth continue to struggle with accepting their gender identity and gaining the acceptance of families and peers. The Internet and increased attention to transgender people in the news media and popular culture have made it possible for young people who think that they might be transgender to learn about the topic readily and to meet transgender people virtually if not in person, but embracing a transgender identity can still be difficult. For example, Martin, a white eighteen-year-old interviewee, feels that he was in denial about being transsexual throughout his childhood and early adolescence. He had to face the issue, though, when he learned that he would be required, as a member of his high school band, to wear a dress during concerts. Martin had nightmares about the situation every night until he admitted to himself the source of his anxiety. Another young participant, "Abe," likewise suppressed her gender identity while growing up and did not begin to accept herself as a woman until she entered college and was free to search for information related to her gender identity. As a former football player, Abe was concerned about "how female [she] really was," which contributed to her initial reluctance to embrace her identity. Unlike Martin and Abe, Paige recognized her transsexual identity in childhood and found supportive information and people online. Still, she did not meet another transgender person "in real life" until recently, when she was eighteen years old.

UNCERTAINTY ABOUT ONE'S GENDER

A majority of the FTM/transgender, MTF/transgender, and male-to-different-gender respondents to our survey began to feel uncertain about the gender assigned to them before the age of thirteen. At the time, most did not have a name for what they were feeling; they simply recognized that the gender that had been attributed to them was wrong or did not completely fit. Another study that looked specifically at the experiences of transgender youth found that they "first became aware that their gender identity or gender expression did not correspond to their biological sex" between six and fifteen years old, with a mean age of 10.4 (Grossman & D'Augelli 2006:120).

The female-to-different-gender participants were less likely to feel gender different as children than the other transgender groups (70 versus 84 percent), and were also less likely to begin to feel uncertain about the gender assigned to them at a young age (35 versus

55 percent). The follow-up interviews suggest that this difference results from the cultural space, often afforded to children assigned female at birth, to assume some traditionally male roles and behavior. Allowed to be "tomboys" by their families at least until puberty—and, unlike most of the FTM/transgender participants, not feeling an overwhelming sense of themselves as male—many female-to-different-gender respondents did not feel out of place or uncertain about the gender assigned to them until their teenage years, when they were frequently expected to act more traditionally feminine.

One of the interviewees who had this experience was Sam, a thirty-three-year-old genderqueer person. Ze thought of hirself as different from other female-assigned children growing up but did not see hirself as the same as boys either. Not knowing that there were options beyond identifying as a boy or a girl, ze considered hirself to be a tomboy and a "part-time kind of girl." Sam did not present as extremely masculine, so hir parents did not initially object to hir gender expression. As long as ze went along with hir mother on some aspects of hir appearance, they tolerated hir behavior. The pressure to conform to gender expectations, though, became worse when ze began high school. Sam "pushed as far as [ze] thought [ze] could without being punished" by hir family and peers.

A "TOMBOY" MOMENT

Whereas majorities in each of our study's four oldest age groups (twenty-three to thirty-two, thirty-three to forty-two, forty-three to fifty-two, and fifty-three and over) began to feel uncertain about their gender identity before age thirteen, only 40 percent of the participants in the eighteen-and-younger age group did so. This "delay" in questioning their gender assignment may be explained by most of the youngest survey participants being female-assigned individuals who identify today as other than female; many of them grew up being able to challenge gender norms without calling into question their own gender. These individuals were commonly perceived as tomboys by their families. As a result, they could often engage in traditionally masculine behavior in childhood without reproach and were not required to see themselves as different from the boys around them.

In the follow-up phone and face-to-face interviews, most (89 percent) of the FTM respondents indicated that they expressed their gender in more "masculine" ways as children, and more than half of these individuals' families were either lenient or did not push them very hard to be more stereotypically female. Anthony, a twenty-eight-year-old white transsexual man, was allowed to be a tomboy as a child; he played largely with other boys and pursued traditionally masculine interests. When he did spend time with girls, he assumed male roles, such as being the husband and father while "playing house." Anthony's mother tried to feminize him by encouraging him to wear dresses, but she did not insist, only "nudging [him] in that direction." She did draw the line on accepting Anthony's masculine behavior when he began to date women in high school who considered him a man, but she changed her mind completely after learning about transsexuality. Another interviewee, Nathan, a forty-nine-year-old African American transsexual man, "didn't have to be anything" growing up and was allowed by his mother to engage in traditionally male activities and roles. The adults in his family also prevented his two sisters and his cousins from picking on him or saying anything about his more masculine gender expression. Adrien, a thirty-five-year-old white FTM participant, was so masculine as a child that his mother went to a psychiatrist when he was about two years old to ask if he could be lesbian. Adrien's family nicknamed him "Patty Hearst" when he was young because he wanted to play with guns and dress as a boy. His mother "did her best to counteract it, but she knew it was a hopeless battle." She gave up challenging his male gender identity and allowed him to dress as he desired.

Other studies of transsexual men have likewise found that many were able to assume traditionally masculine roles growing up, at least until they reached adolescence. Nearly three-fourths of the FTM individuals interviewed by Aaron Devor (1997a) had "very strong commitments to masculine behaviour patterns even as young children" (171), and "in more than one-quarter of their families, these interests were shrugged off as harmless tomboyism and indulged much of the time" (102). Few of the participants' parents engaged in ongoing efforts to eliminate the "masculine" behavioral traits, perhaps because they assumed that their children would grow out of it as teenagers. When conflicts over gender expression arose, it was typically with their mothers. Seven (16 percent) of the respondents to Devor's study indicated that their mothers had been highly critical of them as children for resisting or failing to measure up to feminine standards.

Henry Rubin (2003) finds that the transsexual men in his study identified in one of three ways before puberty: as boys who enjoyed typically boy activities, as tomboys who felt themselves to be different from other female-assigned children while behaving in traditionally male ways, and as boys who enjoyed typically girl activities. The boy-acting FTM boys were more likely to be stigmatized for not following gender norms in childhood. Yet as female social expectations became stricter during adolescence, the tomboys also encountered pressure to conform to more traditional notions of femininity. The behavior of the female-acting FTM boys did not challenge gender norms growing up, which made it harder for them to be taken seriously when they began to identify as transgender.

BETRAYAL AT PUBERTY

Most of the transsexual participants who did not begin to question their gender assignment as children did so during adolescence as they saw their bodies changing in ways that they often found to be extremely distressing. Puberty was especially devastating for many of the participants classified as female-to-male/transgender and female-to-different-gender. With the onset of menstruation and breast development, they no longer fit in as just "one of the boys" and faced greater difficulties being recognized as male or as not female. For the individuals whose families tolerated or accepted them as tomboys, the loss of their androgynous bodies meant the loss of their masculine social space; as the line between male and female became more strictly drawn, these individuals realized that they were being placed on the "wrong" side.

Like other participants who were assigned female at birth, Adrien began to feel uncomfortable with his body at puberty. He "always knew [he] didn't want breasts" and hated them from the day that they began to develop, considering them his "enemy." Many FTM interviewees also indicated a strong aversion to the onset of menstruation. When "Kody," a twenty-four-year-old transgender interviewee, started his period, he remembers telling his mother that he wanted a hysterectomy. His parents were not supportive at the time, but they helped Kody pay for hormone replacement therapy and for top surgery (chest reconstruction to remove breasts) years later after recognizing how important it was for Kody to have a more male-looking body. Puberty was even more traumatic for Robert, who suffered from "suicidal depression" during his first menses and each time thereafter until he reached menopause. He knew that he was a boy from early childhood, but he did not transition until his late forties because the people around him kept insisting that he was female.

Some of the MTF/T and MTDG respondents also experienced a crisis at puberty. "When I was about six, I knew something was wrong, and about age ten, I knew I wanted to be a girl," remembers Jennifer S. But "it wasn't until I reached puberty, and physical changes began, that I understood how disappointed I was and that I felt 'cheated' that I wasn't female." Another MTF participant, Shelby, likewise felt betrayed at puberty. She "thought for sure [she] had female hormones coursing through [her] body and that [she] would develop breasts." Shelby did not understand what she was experiencing until a year or two later, when she saw media coverage of Renée Richards, a transsexual woman who successfully fought to play women's professional tennis.

For the most part, the cross-dressing (CD) individuals we surveyed did not want to change their bodies permanently to look more female; however, a few of the CD interviewees still experienced a profound sense of loss when their bodies began to virilize. Melissa, a white forty-three-year-old cross-dresser, "knew there was something drastically wrong" when she reached puberty. She states: "I became fascinated with women's clothing and much more comfortable wearing women's clothes than men's. I was more interested in being like the girls than I was in dating girls. It became more clear that I was actually a female in a male's body."

Some of the transsexual female and male respondents who initially questioned their gender assignment subsequently repressed their sense of gender difference when faced with opposition from their families. This period of denial was more common among the MTF individuals interviewed, as parents were generally less willing to tolerate expressions of femininity by their seemingly male children than masculinity by their seemingly female children. Nearly twice the percentage of transsexual female than transsexual male interviewees (42 versus 22 percent) indicated that they tried to fit into expected gender roles and denied their "true selves" until sometime in adulthood. Teri, a white forty-two-year-old MTF participant, had fought against her sense of being female since recognizing a desire to cross-dress and play with dolls at about six years old. She came from a Pentecostal family in which traditional gender roles were strictly enforced, and Teri was told from a young age that cross-gender identities were immoral and sinful. She became a mechanic and attained large biceps to try to convince herself and others of her masculinity. However, after developing debilitating ulcers and attempting suicide, she realized that she had to address her underlying feminine feelings or "would end up dead."

Allison, a fifty-year-old Japanese American MTF respondent, also engaged in hypermasculine behavior in response to pressure from her parents. She described how the eldest male in traditional Japanese culture is expected to be the patriarch and carry on the family name and heritage; because she was the oldest male-assigned child, Allison felt obligated to fulfill these roles. As a teenager, she gave in to the expectation that she act in traditionally masculine ways and even went so far as joining the Airborne Rangers after college. She thought that "jumping out of planes would prove [she was] male." By her forties, Allison recognized that she was unhappy with her life as a man and began to seek out other transgender people. Another MTF participant, Kim D., refused to accept that she was transgender for thirty-four years, during which time "[her] life was wrought with alcoholism, substance abuse, and absolute self-hate." Discovering other transgender people via the Internet "eventually saved [her] life, but not before [she] went through many more battles with [her]self."

Some of the transsexual male participants also related stories of feeling forced to assume traditional female gender roles by their families, particularly by their mothers. Michael W.'s mother tried hard to make him as feminine as she could. To please her, he assumed a "sorority-girl appearance" in high school and even entered a junior miss pageant. He gradually became more masculine in his gender expression when he left home to attend college. Kand, a white, nontransitioning FTM interviewee, "went into denial about feeling male when he was a young, preschool-aged, child." He had announced to his mother that he wanted to be a boy, to which she responded by threatening to replace all of his typically male toys with dolls and to make him wear dresses and have long hair adorned with ribbons. In a panic to maintain the limited male/nonfemale space that he had enjoyed, Kand told her that he "didn't really want to be a boy" and thereafter repressed his gender feelings for several decades.

INITIALLY IDENTIFYING AS SOME OTHER IDENTITY

Feeling different from others of their assigned gender eventually led all of the participants to realize that the gender attributed to them was not who they were, or at least not all of who they were. But many of the respondents, especially those who grew up in the 1940s through 1980s, initially did not understand their experiences or have the appropriate language to describe them, leading many to remain confused or to mischaracterize their identities. In particular, older heterosexual FTM individuals frequently first considered themselves to be butch lesbians, and older MTF individuals often first thought that they were cross-dressers.

For many of the heterosexual FTM individuals in the study, identifying as butch lesbians initially satisfied their desire to date women and dress and present in more traditionally masculine ways. Over time, however, they felt uncomfortable with this identity because they recognized that they were much more male than the butch lesbians around them and discovered or learned more about FTM individuals (most had only known about individuals assigned male at birth who transitioned to female). For example, Ted, a thirty-nine-year-old white interviewee, came out as a "dyke" at around sixteen years old because it "was an easy way to explain how [he] didn't fit in" as a masculine, female-bodied individual. He "worked very hard to be a good dyke," which included internalizing the dominant lesbian feminist ideology of the 1970s that considered transsexual men to be identifying with "the oppressor." During his early thirties, Ted began to question this way of thinking and to recognize how he was denying his sense of himself as male. When his ex-lover began to transition, he "couldn't ignore [how he felt] anymore." Another FTM interviewee in his thirties, Lincoln, had identified as butch until he mentioned to a group of butch friends "how great it was that they could hide out as women." The lesbians told him that they felt like and enjoyed being women, and they suggested that Lincoln educate himself about the experiences of transgender people.

Many of the MTF participants began to recognize themselves as female through cross-dressing, so it is not surprising that some thought that they were simply cross-dressers and not transsexual people. Some also did not want to believe that they were transsexual, fearing how it would affect their lives. Shelby "always knew deep down that [she was] female," but it was easier to see herself as a cross-dresser. "I was trying so hard to fit in," she states. Jacqueline first saw herself as a cross-dresser because she "was terrified of surgery, even though [she] wanted it from an early age." But as Jacqueline learned more about transsexuality, she was no longer content with simply cross-dressing. For LuLu, being seen as a woman when she began to cross-dress publicly "opened a Pandora's Box, and [she] couldn't go back" to merely occasional cross-dressing. She tried to live part-time as a woman for a while, but found that it was not enough.

Before people can begin to think that they might be transgender, they must recognize themselves as being different from those around them and begin to question the "normalness" of gender: that someone assigned female at birth is not necessarily female and that someone assigned male at birth is not necessarily male. Clearly, they must also become aware of transgenderism, even if they lack a complete understanding of the concept. It is therefore not surprising that relatively few of the respondents began to think of themselves as transgender before their teens, and only slight majorities in each gender identity category (57 percent of MTF/T participants, 51 percent of FTM/T participants, 51 percent of MTDG participants, and 50 percent of FTDG participants) did so during their teenage years.

Among the interviewees, Andy, a twenty-year-old Asian American woman, initially came out as a gay man in seventh grade because it seemed to make sense; after all, she was a male-bodied individual attracted to men. She became aware of transgender issues in high school through being involved with a local GLSEN (Gay, Lesbian and Straight Education Network) chapter and began to identify as a transgender woman. Another participant now in his twenties, Gavriel, is an Iranian American man who was perceived as a "big brother" by other FTM youth in his high school—even though he did not self-identify as transgender and resisted their attempts to have him attend a transgender support group. He finally attended a Transgender 101 workshop but, still refusing to acknowledge his gender identity, told himself that he was going as an "ally." At the workshop, however, Gavriel saw transgender people like himself, individuals who were neither hypermasculine men nor hyperfeminine women. This experience led him to overcome his denial. Gavriel "needed to meet people who didn't ascribe to gender essentialism" in order to recognize himself.

Studies focusing specifically on gender-nonconforming youth have found that most begin to see themselves as transgender in their early to mid-teenage years. Those interviewed by Arnold Grossman and Anthony D'Augelli (2006) first identified as transgender at a mean age of 14.3 years, several years after they first recognized that their gender identity was incongruent with their gender assignment. In another study of transgender youth (Grossman et al. 2005), the MTF interviewees considered themselves transgender at an average age of 13.4 years and the FTM interviewees at an average age of 15.2 years.

Although most members of the younger age groups in our survey began to wonder if they were transgender before their twenties, many of the older participants did not acknowledge their gender identity until later in life. In particular, 28 percent of those forty-three to fifty-two years old and 35 percent of those older than fifty-two did not consider that they might be transgender until at least age forty. Growing up before the advent of the Internet, and before there was much written about transgender people or much coverage in popular culture, they typically had little or no understanding of their feelings—often thinking there was something wrong with them or that they were "the only one." "Without information, you think you are crazy," states Roxanne, an MTF participant in her fifties. "You are told you are male and you believe the authorities in your life for a while. Although I wanted to be female, I did not have any role model, path, or information to help me understand there were choices I could make." As a consequence, Roxanne "spent years in denial and secret dressing" until she won first prize for cross-dressing in a Halloween costume contest and could no longer ignore her feelings.

Amy, another transgender woman in her fifties, echoes Roxanne. It was "a hopeless situation back then," she remembers; there was little material published on transsexuality, and what was available was highly stigmatizing. Although Amy recognized that she wanted to be female by the time she was nine years old, she did not think that there was anything she could do about it and so "settled into an existence." Not wanting to hurt anyone else, she hid her feelings from her family and friends for decades and never married. Amy's life began to change only when she started talking with other MTF individuals online and realized that transitioning was possible, even in her fifties. It was "the first time that [she] didn't feel alone."

Many of the survey respondents began to think of themselves as transgender before they had met other transgender people. Among the participants interviewed by e-mail, two-thirds stated that they did not know another transgender individual personally when they first assumed that identity. Many had learned about Christine Jorgensen, Renée Richards, and other transsexual people through the media or research, but they did not know how to meet such individuals. D'Anne, a white fifty-seven-year-old MTF interviewee, heard of Jorgensen—the first transsexual celebrity—when she was growing up in the 1950s. She believes that this awareness "kept [her] alive through the early years. Just knowing that it could happen for one person was the piece of hope that [she] clung to for many years." D'Anne did not meet other transgender people until she encountered Mahu[1] sex workers on the streets of Honolulu in her mid-twenties.

Among the different transgender groups surveyed, the female-identified respondents were the most likely to lack transgender friends and acquaintances when they first came out. Whereas 55 percent of the FTM e-mail interviewees indicated that they knew another transgender person before they saw themselves as transgender, only 33 percent of the MTF and 20 percent of the cross-dressing e-mail interviewees did. This difference was also reflected in the larger study, which asked participants when they first met another transgender person. Forty-eight percent of the female-to-male/transgender and 51 percent of the female-to-different-gender respondents had met another transgender person before they were twenty years old, as compared with 14 percent of the male-to-female/transgender and 17 percent of the male-to-different-gender respondents. Thirteen percent of the FTM/T participants even knew another transgender individual before they were teenagers—an experience shared by just 1 percent of the MTF/T participants.

In addition to having relatively earlier contact with other transgender people, the male-identified and nonfemale-identified individuals who were surveyed also learned about transgender people at a generally younger age. Asked when they began to know that they were not alone in being transgender, 60 percent of the FTM/T and 67 percent of the FTDG participants stated that they had discovered there were other transgender people before they were twenty years old, as compared with 48 percent of the MTF/T and 53 percent of the MTDG participants.

Given the greater visibility of female-identified transgender people in popular culture, and given the existence of many more support groups for transsexual women and female-presenting cross-dressers than for male-identified transgender people, these findings may seem counterintuitive. But the results are understandable when one considers that the male-identified participants were significantly younger overall than the female-identified participants. The younger respondents were much more likely to know about and to know other transgender people by the time they self-identified as transgender. Among the more than 300 e-mail interviewees, 69 percent of the eighteen- to twenty-two-year-olds had met another transgender person before they came out themselves, as compared with 38 percent of the twenty-three- to thirty-two-year-olds, 35 percent of the thirty-three- to forty-two-year-olds, 34 percent of the forty-three- to fifty-two-year-olds, and 26 percent of the individuals fifty-three and older. Obviously, participants who were younger than twenty-three had to be aware of transgender people at a young age or else they could not have taken part in the study. Yet even when this group is excluded, our findings demonstrate a relationship between age and transgender awareness. For example, survey respondents who indicated that they knew about other transgender people before the age of twenty included 51 percent of the twenty-three- to thirty-two-year-olds, 41 percent of the thirty-three- to forty-two-year-olds, 34 percent of the forty-three- to fifty-two-year-olds, and 30 percent of those aged fifty-three years and older.

The age of the survey respondents also correlated with when they first met another transgender individual. By age twenty, 32 percent of the nineteen- to twenty-two-year-olds had known another transgender person, as compared with 15 percent of the twenty-three- to thirty-two-year-olds, 10 percent of the thirty-three- to forty-two-year-olds, 8 percent of the forty-three- to fifty-two-year-olds, and

5 percent of those fifty-three years and older. At the other extreme, 35 percent of the thirty-three- to forty-two-year-olds, 48 percent of the forty-three- to fifty-two-year-olds, and 57 percent of those fifty-three and over did not meet another transgender person until they were at least forty years old. In short, the older the participant, the less likely that person was to have had access to transgender people and resources at a young age.

IMPORTANCE OF THE INTERNET

The interviewees who did not know about or meet other transgender people before they were in their forties or older often recounted feeling isolated for many years—until the rise of the Internet enabled them to find resources and a community online. The experiences of Julianne are indicative of technology's influence on resources about and for transgender people. When she was in college in the late 1960s, Julianne researched transsexuality and tranvestism in her university's library but found little beyond old articles about Christine Jorgensen. More than thirty years later, when she bought a computer and connected to the Internet, she "was surprised to learn how many [transgender] resources there were and how many people identified and had similar histories and feelings to [her] own. This marked the beginning of a process which led [her] to support groups, both virtual and real, counseling, and the path to transition."

The contacts that many older respondents established through the Internet made it possible for them to accept and more openly express their gender identity. For example, Rachel B. overcame her fears of letting other people see her as a woman, as well as her growing sense of hopelessness, with the help of the other transsexual women she met online. Realizing that she could successfully and happily transition, Rachel "finally faced up to [her] denial." Leigh, a white cross-dresser over fifty years old, also came out because of the support she received online. "Without the Internet, I have no idea where I'd be in this process," she states. "Undoubtedly, still in hiding." Another cross-dresser, Tina S., sums up the sentiments of many: "I learned from reading, but I was *liberated* by the Internet!"

The importance of the Internet in the lives of many of the participants was reflected in how they first met other transgender people. Among the e-mail respondents, the Internet was a primary method by which members of each age group (except for those older than fifty-three) came to know other people like themselves. The participants in the oldest age bracket relied twice as often (35 versus 17.5 percent) on support groups as on online venues to begin meeting others. In contrast, individuals in their teens, twenties, and thirties initially encountered other transgender people more often through having transgender friends and acquaintances, as well as through the Internet.

Because our research involved an online survey, the study was likely biased toward individuals who have used the Internet to understand themselves and gain support. However, our results parallel other, non-Web-based studies that indicate the Internet plays a significant role in the lives of many transgender people. Darryl Hill (2005) conducted in-depth interviews with twenty-eight transgender-identified people in Toronto, Canada. Eighteen respondents were interviewed in 1996 and nine were reinterviewed five years later along with ten additional participants. Hill found that the majority of the interviewees "relied on technology to come to terms with their gender, connect with others like themselves, and develop a more sophisticated sense of issues facing their community either by raising their consciousness or helping them to tell their own story" (49). Through meeting other transgender people virtually, they learned about transgender identities and felt less isolated. Eve Shapiro (2004) reaches a similar conclusion following interviews with ten U.S. transgender activists. She finds that online communities have largely replaced traditional support groups as sites for networking, making meaning of one's experiences, and collective identity development for the growing number of transgender people coming out publicly today. Further examining the ways in which technologies are (re)shaping gendered identities, Shapiro (2010) traces how "Internet use has helped individuals learn, practice, and adopt new gender identity scripts, learn about whether and how to shape their body as authentic transgender individuals, and has offered new—and often more accepting—social gender paradigms" (108). For example, the Internet has been critical to the growth and visibility of a greater diversity of transgender identities, including gay FTMs, drag kings, genderqueers, and other gender-nonconforming individuals.

Shapiro (2004) cites the tremendous number of websites focused on transgender issues—a basic online search she performed in 2002 revealed more than 800,000 pages—as evidence of the extent to which transgender people have made use of the Internet. Online transgender resources have become even more expansive since that time. On August 21, 2010, a search on Google for "transgender" yielded about 12.8 million results. The term "gender identity" returned nearly 9.8 million sites.

Still, as Samons (2009) points out, it would be a mistake to assume that all transgender people can now take advantage of online resources, or of the growing media coverage of transgender issues, to learn about and better understand their experiences. Although noting that the transgender people she sees today are typically more open about their gender identity and less in need of basic transgender information than a decade ago, Samons describes how some of her clients continue to have little or no awareness of the transgender community when they approach her for therapy. These individuals may not have Internet access, may lack privacy when going online, or may be too scared to seek transgender information for fear that a spouse or family member will somehow find the material on their computer.

SOCIALIZING WITH OTHER TRANSGENDER PEOPLE

Many of the survey respondents initially relied on the Internet to make contact with others like themselves, but most subsequently sought to meet and develop friendships with other transgender people. More than one-third of the FTM/T and MTF/T participants socialized "often" or "very often" with other transgender individuals. About another third of both groups "sometimes" did so, while only 6 and 10 percent, respectively, indicated that they "never" spent time with other people whom they know to be transgender. Similar findings result when respondents are grouped by age. Between 30 and 40 percent of the members in each age group (except for those younger than nineteen) socialized "often" or "very often" with other transgender people. Slightly fewer participants (28 percent) in the youngest age group socialized regularly with other transgender individuals. This finding may reflect that, on average, these youth had been out as transgender for less time than had many of the older participants and therefore had experienced less contact with the transgender community. Those who live with their parents or other family members who are unaware or unsupportive of their transgender identities may also have limited opportunities to socialize with other transgender people.

Between 9 and 12 percent of each age group indicated that they never spend time with people whom they know to be transgender. The reasons participants chose not to do so varied. For some, it was because they were not open about being transgender or having a transgender past and feared being in situations that might cause their gender identity to be questioned. Others had completely transitioned and no longer identified as transgender, so did not feel a need to be around transgender people. Some respondents wanted to spend time with other transgender people but had few chances to do so because they lived in rural areas. Trish, a white cross-dresser in her sixties, was one of the interviewees faced with this situation. She lives in a small town where she knows no one like herself and where there is no place she can safely go cross-dressed. As a result, Trish cross-dresses only at home and when attending conferences of Tri-Ess (the Society for the Second Self), a national organization for heterosexual male cross-dressers and their partners.

Unlike Trish, the respondents who lived in urban areas often had many opportunities to socialize with other transgender people— whether through participating in transgender-specific events or groups or simply because they have transgender friends and acquaintances. Grossman and D'Augelli's (2006) study of transgender youth in the New York City area demonstrates the possibilities provided by a large city. Fifty-four percent of the participants reported that they spend time daily with other transgender people, while another 44 percent do so on a weekly basis.

In each gender identity category and in each age group, a majority of the respondents who interacted with other transgender people did so through social activities. These activities ranged from regular, organized events—such as Fantasia Fair in Provincetown, Massachusetts, the Southern Comfort Conference in Atlanta, and "Girls' Night Out" groups around the country—to informal gatherings of friends. For many of the cross-dressing participants, these events were their main opportunity to present as female in public. Trish, for example, had not met many other cross-dressers or had the chance to cross-dress publicly until she became involved in Tri-Ess functions. Being with other cross-dressers, she says, "liberated [her] to be [her]self." She could "talk football and pantyhose" and be accepted. Another interviewee, Sandra, first went out in public cross-dressed at a Southern Comfort Conference and found it to be a transformative experience. Writing on her website (www .gendertree.com), she states, "my overwhelming feeling was being completely comfortable as Sandra for four days."

Significant numbers of the MTF/T participants (57 percent) and FTM/T participants (52 percent) spent time with other transgender people while seeking personal support. Michael W., for example, organized a transsexual male support group as he was considering transitioning. His partner at the time accompanied him to the first meeting and told Michael that "you had been there ten minutes and you felt at home." He started to transition shortly thereafter. Jennifer Z. also cites her involvement with a support group as being instrumental in her process of transitioning. She went from being uncertain about whether she could transition to leading the group's meeting for transitioning members two years later.

As compared with the MTF/transgender and FTM/transgender participants, fewer of the female- and male-to-different-gender participants (42 and 39 percent, respectively) socialized in the context of receiving support from other transgender individuals or from organized groups. This difference is not surprising given that transgender support groups have historically been geared toward individuals who transition to or who present as male or female and not toward individuals who identify and/or express their gender in nonbinary ways. In the last ten to fifteen years, some support groups have become more inclusive in response to the rapidly growing number of transgender people, especially transgender youth, who see themselves as neither male nor female, as both, or as somewhere in between (Bolin 1994). But individuals who challenge a male-female dichotomy still feel out of place in many long-standing support groups. For example, Stephe—a white, male-assigned individual who identifies as androgyne or third gender—once regularly dressed in "women's" clothing publicly. Ze stopped doing so, however, because "people didn't get it," including the members of the support group ze attended. According to Stephe, only two of the fifteen regulars understood hir.

Other study participants who express their gender in nonbinary ways also indicated that they were often not accepted by transgender people who are more gender typical. 'Ron, a multiracial, twenty-eight-year-old genderqueer individual, stated that some transgender people see hir identity as a "new fad." As a result, ze has been more comfortable developing hir identity on hir own. Like 'Ron, Caiden, a twenty-one-year-old college student, has not received much support from transgender people who believe in a gender dichotomy. Hir main source of support has been a friend who similarly "identifies in the gray area" of gender.

In addition to having a limited appreciation of gender diversity, most support groups outside of college and youth settings still consist primarily of transsexual men, transsexual women, or female-presenting cross-dressers in their forties and older. As a result, many younger transgender people do not join or remain in traditional support groups, often preferring to connect online. Fewer of the respondents (47–51 percent) in our study who were younger than thirty-three socialized through support groups than did older individuals (55–60 percent). The contrast was even sharper when age was broken down further. Among the e-mail interviewees who were at least fifty-three years old, the percentage who met other transgender people through support groups was nearly twice as high (35 versus 18 percent) as that of eighteen- to twenty-two-year-olds who did so.

In the context of political activism, however, the younger individuals surveyed were more likely than were the older respondents to socialize with other transgender people. The FTM/T and FTDG participants, a majority of whom were less than twenty-three years old, were especially likely to spend time with others through their advocacy for transgender rights and other issues. Thirty-eight percent of the FTM/T participants and 48 percent of the FTDG participants socialized politically with other transgender people, as compared with 24 and 26 percent of the MTF/T and MTDG participants, respectively.

The respondents engaged in many different forms of activism that placed them in contact with other transgender people. Some had visible political roles as leaders of national, state, or local transgender or LGBT (lesbian, gay, bisexual, and transgender) organizations. Others participated in these groups or the events they sponsor, such as conferences, lobby days, and observances of the Transgender Day of Remembrance—an annual event held to commemorate the lives of people murdered because of their gender identity/expression.

For some, political activism involved a personal struggle. Jake, for example, became an outspoken advocate for transgender rights after he was denied the right to marry his wife in Ohio. The jurisdiction in which he sought to obtain a marriage license refused to recognize him as a man even though Jake had legally changed the gender on his birth certificate to reflect his male identity. Because Jake was assigned female at birth, the judge considered the marriage to be between two people of the same sex, which is banned in Ohio. Jake and his wife sought to have the case overturned, but an appellate court reaffirmed the initial decision. Rather than potentially setting a negative legal precedent, Jake and his wife did not appeal to the Ohio Supreme Court; instead, they married in another state and moved to a different city.

Other survey participants became activists after they encountered job discrimination. Despite having a master's degree in criminal justice, Ted, an FTM interviewee, was unable to obtain work in the field because his transgender past would inevitably be disclosed during background checks and lead to his rejection. He decided to come out more publicly and took a job with his state's health department, where he was placed in charge of a statewide transgender health initiative that included conducting a transgender needs assessment, coordinating trainings for health care providers, and creating a resource and referral service for transgender people.

Whether through political, social, or support activities, the participants who chose to spend time with other transgender people indicated that they learned more about being transgender and benefited psychologically from interacting with individuals who shared or could relate to their experiences and who could serve as role models. For example, Michelle L., a Latina interviewee who identifies as "somewhere between transsexual and a cross-dresser," credits being involved with several support groups as helping her to understand her identity and "to see there are many options between being closeted and having surgery to become female." Julie Marie met her first transsexual friend through a support group, and because she is not yet open about her gender identity to her family or nontransgender friends, she relies on members of the group for understanding and assurance.

COMING OUT TO OTHERS

In their study of masculine-to-feminine transgender people, Gagné et al. (1997) recognize an important difference between the coming out experiences of many transsexual women and many female-presenting cross-dressers. Because the MTF individuals were making a permanent and highly visible life change, they could not restrict who would know. They often began by telling their romantic partners and then close family members whom they thought might be supportive, but eventually everyone around them would find out. In contrast, the cross-dressers could limit disclosure and typically came out only to their partners and other transgender people.

Yet the cross-dressers who participated in our survey, and particularly those who accepted our invitation to be interviewed, were often quite public about their cross-dressing. Consequently, they tended to be out to at least some friends (see table 2.1), family members (tables 2.2 and 2.3), and coworkers (table 2.4) as well as to their partners. Julie, for example, has come out to most of her family and, because she presents as female in her day-to-day life, is known as a cross-dresser in her neighborhood, at her children's school, and at her church. She finds that members of her Unitarian Universalist congregation are welcoming, but most of her neighbors "pretty much hate [her]," and one of her children has been confronted at school with why her father dresses as a woman.

The interviewees who identified as genderqueer or as other nonbinary gender identities also were frequently very open to the

TABLE 2.1 Level of outness to friends by gender identity

| Level of Outness | Gender Identity | | | | | | | |
| | FTM/T | | FTDG | | MTF/T | | MTDG | |
	%	n	%	n	%	n	%	n
Out to all friends	39.8	260	28.8	30	28.1	613	17.8	27
Out to most friends	30.2	197	16.3	17	14.9	324	14.5	22
Out to some friends	14.2	93	20.2	21	14.2	310	13.2	20
Out to only a few close friends	12.3	80	24.0	25	26.9	585	25.0	38
Totally closeted to friends	3.1	20	8.7	9	15.3	333	27.6	42

Notes: A majority (70 percent) of the FTM/T respondents were out to all or most of their friends, as compared with less than half (43 percent) of the MTF/T respondents. Although relatively few (9 percent) of the FTDG respondents were totally closeted, overall they reported being out to fewer friends than did the FTM/T respondents. The MTF/T and MTDG respondents tended to be either completely out or totally (or almost totally) closeted. At 28 percent, the MTDG respondents were the most closeted of all groups.

Level of Outness	Gender Identity							
	FTM/T		FTDG		MTF/T		MTDG	
	%	n	%	n	%	n	%	n
Out to all nuclear family members	57.9	378	27.9	29	42	914	28.9	44
Out to most nuclear family members	11.0	72	9.6	10	8.7	189	6.6	10
Out to some nuclear family members	5.5	36	7.7	8	5.8	127	8.6	13
Out to only a few close nuclear family members	10.7	70	16.3	17	19.9	434	19.1	29
Totally closeted to all nuclear family members	14.2	93	36.5	38	23.1	503	34.2	52

Notes: The FTM/T participants were much more out to nuclear family members than were the other groups: 69 percent (versus 36–51 percent) were out to all or most of their immediate families. The FTDG participants were almost evenly divided between individuals who were completely or mostly out to nuclear family members (38 percent) and individuals who were totally closeted (37 percent). The MTDG participants were likewise about evenly divided between those who were largely out (36 percent) and those who were entirely closeted (34 percent). In general, the MTF/T participants were less out than the FTM/T participants but more out than the MTDG and FTDG participants.

people in their lives. Like the transsexual respondents, many had no choice about disclosure because they had transitioned in whole or in part or otherwise presented full-time outside of the gender assigned to them at birth. The genderqueer participants who were not perceived as transgender were still often out to people whom they met because they did not want to reinforce a gender binary. One of the genderqueer interviewees who felt this way was Aaron H., a white thirty-two-year-old. Although he is usually seen by others as male because he has had top surgery and taken testosterone for almost a decade, Aaron rejects the idea that not being female means that he identifies as male. Recognizing the fluidity of gender, he characterizes his identity "as a process and not as an end point."

Likewise, some of the transsexual interviewees who had completely transitioned and are able to "pass" frequently disclosed

TABLE 2.3 Level of outness to extended family by gender identity

	Gender Identity							
	FTM/T		FTDG		MTF/T		MTDG	
Level of Outness	%	n	%	n	%	n	%	n
Out to all extended family	25.3	165	7.7	8	22.5	489	12.5	19
Out to most extended family	15.6	102	3.8	4	9.4	205	7.2	11
Out to some extended family	9.8	64	12.5	13	9.1	198	9.2	14
Out to only a few close extended family members	14.4	94	16.3	17	12.6	275	12.5	19
Totally closeted to extended family	33.1	216	57.7	60	45.2	984	55.9	85

Notes: The FTM/T respondents were divided between being out to all or most extended family members (41 percent) and being largely or totally closeted (57 percent). Large majorities of the FTDG (87 percent), MTF/T (67 percent), and MTDG (78 percent) respondents reported being largely or totally closeted to extended family members.

their transgender histories to new people in their lives. Even though they may identify as women or men and no longer consider themselves transgender, they feel that their transgender experiences constitute an important part of their pasts. Andre is one of the FTM participants who has no desire to "pass as a man." Having passed as female and repressed his sense of himself as transgender until he was in his forties, Andre does not want to have to hide who he is again.

COMING OUT TO THEIR PARTNERS

Almost all of the people we interviewed were out to their partners as transgender. Some, though, were not open when the relationships began because they feared the person would not want to be involved with them, because they hoped the relationship would "cure" them, or because they were still in denial about their gender

TABLE 2.4 Level of outness to professional colleagues by gender identity

Level of Outness	Gender Identity							
	FTM/T		FTDG		MTF/T		MTDG	
	%	n	%	n	%	n	%	n
Out to all professional colleagues	19.0	124	13.5	14	19.4	422	11.2	17
Out to most professional colleagues	18.1	118	13.5	14	9.0	195	7.9	12
Out to some professional colleagues	16.2	106	14.4	15	11.0	240	11.2	17
Out to only a few close professional colleagues	19.8	129	16.3	17	17.6	383	12.5	19
Totally closeted to professional colleagues	25.7	168	41.3	43	42.0	915	53.9	82

Notes: Majorities of the FTDG (58 percent), MTF/T (60 percent), and MTDG (66 percent) participants stated that they were out to none of their colleagues or to just a few. The FTM/T participants were more likely to be out, but little more than a third (37 percent) were open about being transgender to all or most of their colleagues.

identity. Tiffany, a white and Vietnamese thirty-three-year old who describes herself as a "part-time girl," had wanted to say something to her wife before they were married but did not know how. She was also just starting to understand herself at that time. It was not until after their marriage began that Tiffany fully realized that she was transgender. Before Tiffany could find a way to tell her wife about her cross-dressing, her wife discovered Tiffany's "women's" clothing. Since neither of them was happy in the marriage, Tiffany's cross-dressing served as a convenient way to end the relationship.

Tiffany's experiences were not uncommon among the married cross-dressing participants in our survey. Many saw their marriages end when they disclosed—or their wives found out—that they cross-dressed; their spouses could not accept the idea that they wore "women's" clothing, or believed that they were actually gay or transsexual despite assurances to the contrary. Some interviewees were able to preserve their relationships even though their wives continued to oppose their cross-dressing. Cheryl's first marriage ended, in part, because of conflicts over her cross-dressing, so she was up front with her second wife about her gender identity before they married. Cheryl's second wife "understands academically" but is not emotionally supportive and remains uncomfortable with Cheryl's need to present as female. The lack of support has been hard for Cheryl, as she "wants to be accepted as a complete person" and not have to hide or deny a basic part of herself.

Some wives sought limits on their spouses' cross-dressing as a condition for remaining in the marriage. A common stipulation was that the cross-dressers not do so in front of the spouse and/or the children. Other cross-dressing interviewees were permitted to present *en femme* inside their homes or out of town but had agreed to restrict their public cross-dressing locally in order to minimize the possibility of disclosure. Ginger has this type of arrangement with her wife. They travel together to places like Key West and Las Vegas, where Ginger can freely cross-dress; however, in the conservative southern city in which they are respected professionals, she cross-dresses only at gay clubs and other venues where she is unlikely to run into people she knows.

Over time, some of the wives became more supportive as they learned about transgender people and recognized that their spouses were not disordered or necessarily about to transition to female. These wives differed from the less accepting partners in that they did not seek to limit their spouses' cross-dressing and, in fact, often accompanied them to cross-dressing events and bought them "women's" clothing. In Tina M.'s case, she and her wife, "Peggy," exchange outfits, as they are the same size. While "Peggy" has not wanted to accompany her out cross-dressed, she is beginning to allow Tina to cross-dress in front of her, which is a tremendous relief to Tina.

The MTF, FTM, and genderqueer participants who were transitioning often encountered even greater difficulties coming out to their partners, since the disclosure dramatically shifted basic assumptions about the nature of their relationships. According to these interviewees, almost all of their partners reacted harshly to the admission, for it not only called into question everything that their partners thought they knew about them, but it also raised concerns about their partners' sexual orientation. Many of the relationships ended because the partners were unwilling to be with someone of a gender different than they had known and/or did not want to be perceived as being involved with someone of the same sex (or of a different sex). Jennifer Z., for example, states that her wife sought a divorce because "she could not handle the thought of being married to a woman," and Adrien's partner left him when he began to transition, deciding that she "didn't want to live with a man." Because his partner identified as bisexual, Adrien had thought that she would be able to adjust to the change. But he realizes now that she was more attracted to women, so it made a huge difference to her when Adrien started to be seen by others as male.

The partners of the FTM participants who identified as lesbians often had an especially hard time coping with the loss of their own identities. For some partners, it had been an arduous process to accept and take pride in themselves as lesbians, and now this hard-won accomplishment was being taken away. Those who were active in lesbian communities also suddenly felt like they no longer had a place to belong and faced potentially huge upheavals in their social, cultural, and political lives. Turner's partner at the time ended their relationship when he changed his name and the pronouns he used; she identified as a lesbian and felt that he was making her invisible. Both Andre and Will indicated that their partners continue to stay in the relationships but are struggling with the effects of their transitions. Andre's partner is very open as a lesbian and is adamant about not being seen by others as a straight woman, while Will's partner is not out and fears the visibility that may result from a change in Will's identity and appearance.

Some of the FTM-lesbian couples were able to get past their struggles. Ryan's partner agreed to his top surgery because she knew how much Ryan hated his breasts, but she wanted him to wait before taking hormones. After what Ryan describes as "a lot of work and a lot of crying," she came to accept his transition and they recently bought a house together.

Similarly, some of the MTF interviewees and their heterosexual spouses found ways to sustain their relationships, even if traditional labels no longer fit. LuLu's wife was frightened when LuLu first told her that she cross-dressed, but the disclosure enabled them "to know each other all over again." When LuLu subsequently raised the idea of transitioning, her wife said that she would "stay with [her] for now." That was more than two years ago. While other people may see them as in "a lesbian relationship," they choose not to define it that way. Her wife still identifies as straight and LuLu as a transgender woman.

Most of the transsexual interviewees whose relationships survived the transition process had told their partners at the outset that they were transgender or had met their partners while they were transitioning. Rachel G.'s wife knew when she married that Rachel cross-dressed and has been very supportive of her transition. They have been married ten years and go together to buy clothes and to attend transgender support group meetings. Nathan indicates that his wife, whom he met just as he was beginning to transition, has also been a primary source of support. She readily saw him as a man, as she had never been attracted to women.

COMING OUT TO THEIR CHILDREN

While the transgender interviewees often received a negative reaction from their partners when they came out, their children were generally supportive. Typical was the response of Liz's son. With the help of a therapist, she told him ten years ago (when he was twelve years old) that she was a transsexual woman. Liz describes the experience as "almost a nonevent." He was more concerned about his parents staying together than about her gender identity. Dan, a forty-eight-year-old FTM participant, also considers the reactions of his three children to have been "very good." They have been "more supportive than [he] gave them credit for."

The cross-dressing interviewees did not face the same need to disclose their gender identity to their children, and some chose not to do so because of how they see their role as a parent. Angie has not come out to her twenty-five-year-old daughter because, as she states, "I'm Dad for her and [don't] want to spoil that." Similarly, Ginger has told neither of her two adult daughters, believing that she "has to be there for them, and there is really no reason to involve them."

The cross-dressing participants who did decide to come out to their children, or whose children discovered them cross-dressed, generally received a positive response. Both of Rae Louise's children found out by accident that she cross-dresses. It did not matter to her son (then seventeen years old), and her daughter (then thirteen) thought it was "kind of cool." They have gone out together, and even attended a wedding, with Rae Louise cross-dressed. Another cross-dressing interviewee, Donna, related the following story. "I once asked my eight-year-old if it bothered her that I was different. She replied—with a wisdom beyond her young age—[by] telling me that being different was okay and that people should be able to be whoever they want to be. It was all I could do to keep from crying. I can only hope that she never loses that view of the world."

Some of the MTF and FTM interviewees waited to disclose, and did not start transitioning, until their children were adults so as not to make their growing up more difficult. Risa, a white fifty-six-year-old transsexual woman, was among the survey participants who postponed transitioning to avoid interfering with her child's life. She states that she wanted to be "Dad" for her daughter until she was on her own. "Carol" likewise held off beginning to take hormones until the last of her three children had left home, a delay of twenty years. When she finally came out to them, they were "very supportive." One of her daughters helped Carol feel comfortable going out publicly as female, and another daughter assisted her in how she dressed and presented herself. In a reversal of roles, Carol says that this daughter "sort of raised me."

Only a few of the transgender interviewees indicated that their children had a sustained negative response to their coming out. Among the most hostile receptions was the reaction to Kaye's disclosure. Kaye, a white sixty-four-year-old MTF participant, had been the director of a fundamentalist mission serving the hungry and homeless before her family discovered that she was transgender and publicly outed her. Because they see Kaye's gender identity as sinful, all but one of her six children refuse to speak to her and, as a result, she has no contact with her eight grandchildren. Her ninety-one-year-old mother was likewise cut off by the family when she supported Kaye.

COMING OUT TO THEIR PARENTS

The acceptance by Kaye's mother was indicative of the experiences of the transsexual interviewees as a whole. Among both the MTF and FTM participants, mothers tended to be more supportive than fathers—perhaps because many of the respondents had been closer to their mothers before they came out. For example, when Mekah came out to her parents, her father did not understand but her mother quickly came to embrace her as female and to see Mekah as their daughter. Bobbie Jean relates how her mother, a seventy-six-year-old Baptist minister, had always thought that she was different. Her response to Bobbie Jean's coming out as a transsexual woman was "What took you so long?"

Some initially antagonistic parents were more supportive over time as they came to recognize that their children had always felt gender different and that continued opposition would not prevent them from transitioning but only alienate them. Such was the case with Jacie's parents. They became more accepting when they understood that Jacie was not going to change; what was going to change was that they would no longer be a part of her life if they remained hostile. Her parents now call her "she" and her mother renamed her "Jacie," the name she would have received had she been assigned female at birth. Michael W.'s mother underwent a similar shift in perspective. Realizing that her son had always been male, she came to see that what mattered most was that he was happy and healthy.

Some parents remained hostile despite attempts by their transgender children to persuade them otherwise. When Ryan explained to his parents that he was transitioning, his mother "cried for months" and his father disowned him, even going as far as to take pictures of him off their walls. For more than a year, they treated Ryan as if he were dead. He finally was able to see his parents recently, but their relationship remains strained. Another participant, Mary, was similarly cut off from her family when she announced that she was planning to transition. Her mother will not let Mary visit her home, and so—although they communicate online and by telephone—Mary has not seen her mother in nearly two years.

The parents who could not accept their children as transsexual were often unable to move beyond feeling that they had somehow caused them to be transgender or that the children they had known had died. Robbi, a white fifty-four-year-old MTF interviewee, states that the only person in her family who remains unsupportive is her father, who thinks "[he] must have done something wrong" in raising Robbi. In Elliot's family, it is his mother who "took it really hard." She "mourns the death of her daughter" and will not call him "Elliot" or use male pronouns unless pressed to do so. Similarly, Patricia states that her mother struggled for about five years, grieving over the "death of her son." Her mother, though, "turned around" when Patricia confronted her and said that if her mother continued to be ashamed of her, Patricia did not want her mother in her life.

SUMMARY OF HOW PARTICIPANTS EXPERIENCED BEING TRANSGENDER

Many of the transgender people surveyed indicated that they became aware in early childhood that how they felt about their gender did not match the gender assigned to them at birth. Some of the participants, especially some of the female-assigned participants, had greater leeway to act outside of traditional gender roles as children. As a result, they did not begin to see themselves as gender different until the onset of puberty, when their bodies began to develop in ways that they often abhorred and, with these changes, gender expectations began to be more strictly enforced. Still, the female-assigned respondents generally continued to have a greater ability to act outside of gender norms than did the male-assigned respondents, many of whom were criticized or punished if their behavior was perceived as feminine in any way.

In response to the social disapproval of gender nonconformity, nearly half of the female transsexual interviewees, and nearly a fourth of the male transsexual interviewees, tried to fit into traditional gender roles and to repress their sense of themselves as gender different. Others embraced another sexual or gender identity as a means to deny that they were transgender or transsexual or because they did not fully comprehend the nature of their feelings. The older respondents were especially likely to have had this experience, given the general lack of resources and information for transgender people prior to the widespread availability of the Internet in the 1990s and 2000s. We found that, among the individuals surveyed who grew up in the 1940s through the 1980s, many of the heterosexual FTM participants identified as butch lesbians and many of the MTF participants identified as cross-dressers before gaining a better understanding of themselves.

The Internet helped respondents of all ages accept and more openly express their gender identity. Through being online, many of the participants learned about and came to know others who shared similar experiences. Most subsequently met and socialized with other transgender people via informal friendship networks, organized support groups, and/or educational, political, or social events. Even individuals who lived where they did not know other transgender people—or did not feel comfortable being out in public—were often able to find others and be open elsewhere via online networking.

Almost all of the individuals we interviewed had disclosed to their partners, if not to others as well, that they identify as transgender. Obviously, participants in the process of completely or partially transitioning could not keep this information from the people in their lives. Yet the vast majority of cross-dressing interviewees had also come out to their partners, and often to their children, because they wanted to share such an important part of themselves with the individuals closest to them.

The reactions of partners varied. Most of the transsexual interviewees reported that their romantic relationships ended once they began to transition, as their partners did not want to be involved with someone of a gender different than what they had known.

The change was less dramatic for partners of the cross-dressing interviewees, and most of these relationships continued even if the partners remained unsupportive of the cross-dressing. Participants who told their partners that they were transgender at the outset of a relationship, or who met partners while they were transitioning, were more likely to have sustained the relationship than were participants who came out to their partners sometime later.

The children and parents of the interviewees tended to be more supportive than their partners, no doubt because the disclosure did not call into question the basic nature of their relationship or the other family members' sexual orientations. The transgender person was still a child or a parent, even if the label of son/daughter or father/mother was changing. In only a few instances did children completely reject their transgender parents; similarly, most parents came to accept their transgender children even if the relationship became strained.

Transgender people often encounter bias when they transition or otherwise come out to or are recognized as transgender by others. This is why the respondents, if they were able to limit disclosure, were generally less willing to be out to individuals beyond their immediate families and perhaps a few close friends.

The next chapter discusses the climate for transgender people today by focusing on the survey participants' experiences with harassment, violence, and employment discrimination. Many of the respondents who could avoid disclosing their gender identity sometimes or often did so because they feared for their safety and sought to minimize the chances that they would experience anti-transgender prejudice.

Phyllis

Sarafina

Loren

Sara

3

THE CLIMATE FOR TRANSGENDER PEOPLE

I have been open to others since the day I decided to quit hiding
in my own life. I have had all the range of responses possible.
From loss of jobs, family, and support systems, violent con-
frontations and refusal of health care, inability to find housing,
discrimination and the like, to some people being supportive and
finally mending some family relationships, making new friends,
and being visible within society at large.

— TERRILYNN

Several terms are used to describe institutional or organizational
contexts, including psychological climate, organizational climate,
and organizational culture (Parker et al. 2003). *Climate* can be
conceptualized both as a perception and as a description (Rousseau 1988), and it has been a focus of organizational research
since the late 1960s (Litwin & Stringer 1968). Later researchers
distinguished between individual and organizational conceptualiza-
tions of climate, labeling them *psychological* and *organizational*
climate, respectively (James & Jones 1974). According to William
Glick (1985), "researchers concerned with individual perceptions
focus on psychological climate, whereas organizational climate is
investigated when organizational attributes are of interest" (602).
Since individual perceptions were of greatest interest in the founda-
tional research for this book, our review will focus on psychological climate.

Psychological climate is frequently measured by considering the
beliefs and experiences of different population groups, including

the perceptions of individuals who are not members of the specific groups being discussed (Bensimon 2004; Hofstede, Neuijen, Ohayv, & Sanders 1990; Hurtado 1992; Rankin 2003). However, a review of climate research reveals a lack of agreement on what is actually meant by psychological climate. Moreover, terms such as "climate," "environment," and "culture" are often used interchangeably, leaving the reader confused about what is being measured. Based on our reading of the literature and several years of experience assessing climate,[1] we understand psychological climate to be the current attitudes, behaviors, and standards of people within an organization, institution, or culture. The literature and our own research also support the notion that one's psychological "safety" is influenced by climate and is a critical factor in one's engagement in society. Individuals experience psychological safety when they feel able to "show and employ one's self without fear of negative consequences to self-image, status, or career" (Kahn 1990:708). Psychological safety is a state that exists across cultures and is evident throughout a wide range of individual differences. People will be personally engaged when they feel psychologically safe to do so. Thus, a climate for psychological safety describes a climate where one feels safe to speak up without being rejected or punished (Baer & Frese 2003).

The quotation that opens this chapter reflects how the societal climate—or the current attitudes, behaviors, standards, and practices of societal institutions (employers, health agencies, etc.)—often discriminate against people who are transgender and thereby create an "unsafe" climate for transgender people. One reason we undertook the research project that forms the foundation of this book was to examine the climate for transgender people in the United States. We were particularly interested in considering the climate for individuals who, within this group that is typically marginalized, are often marginalized further: gender-nonconforming people; transgender people of color; transgender people who are lesbian, gay, or bisexual; and younger and older transgender people.

For the most part, information on the climate for transgender populations is limited to some data on the experiences of transgender college students (Rankin 2003, 2006, 2007; Reason & Rankin

2006) and the more recent survey conducted by the National Gay and Lesbian Task Force and the National Center for Transgender Equality (NGLTF/NCTE 2009) on discrimination in employment, health agencies, and housing. Because the survey we constructed for this project was based on campus climate literature, this chapter proceeds first with a review of the literature on measuring the campus climate and of the findings from this literature with respect to lesbian, gay, bisexual, and transgender people.[2] The balance of the chapter addresses the types and our respondents' experiences of anti-transgender bias, showing how this bias is a logical outgrowth of the genderism prevalent in educational, religious, and governmental institutions.

CAMPUS CLIMATE

As colleges and universities increasingly reflect the diverse makeup of society, institutions have focused on the importance of creating a campus environment that includes, welcomes, and accepts all people and one that responds to issues of diversity (Malaney, Williams, & Gellar 1997; Rankin & Reason 2008; Worthington, Navarro, Loewy, & Hart 2008). Although colleges and universities attempt to foster welcoming and inclusive environments, they are not immune to negative societal attitudes and discriminatory practices. As a microcosm of the larger social environment, college and university campuses reflect the prevailing prejudices of society (Eliason 1996; Nelson & Krieger 1997). Consequently, campus climates have variously been described as "racist" for students and employees of color (Harper & Hurtado 2007; Rankin & Reason 2005), "chilly" for women (Hall & Sandler 1984; Hart & Fellabaum 2008), and "hostile" for lesbian, gay, bisexual, and transgender community members (Eliason 1996; Rankin 2003, 2006).

MEASURING CAMPUS CLIMATE

A number of theoretical models have been developed to conceptualize and describe the campus climate at colleges and universities.

Earlier research focused on the role of attitudes, perceptions, and observations in the campus environment (Milem, Chang, & Antonio 2005). Sylvia Hurtado (1992) introduces a multidimensional framework (further developed by Hurtado, Milem, Clayton-Pederson, & Allen 1998) for understanding campus climate that replaces psychological climate (i.e., perceptions and attitudes) with a more inclusive definition that acknowledges additional factors: impact of the institution's structure and history, interactions among people of different identities, and internal and external forces shaping campus climate (Milem et al. 2005). Specifically, this framework identifies four interrelated dimensions of the campus climate: an institution's historical legacy of inclusion or exclusion of various racial or ethnic groups; structural diversity in terms of the number of racial or ethnic groups represented on campus; psychological climate, consisting of perceptions and attitudes between and among groups; and behavioral climate as characterized by intergroup relations on campus (Hurtado et al. 1998). By developing a comprehensive framework for understanding campus climate, Hurtado (1994) and Hurtado et al. (1998) are able to offer suggestions about "how to improve educational policy and practice through the engagement of campus diversity" (Milem et al. 2005:14).

Building on the work of Smith and colleagues (1997) and Hurtado et al. (1998), Sue Rankin (2003) developed the Transformational Tapestry Model. The model was expanded on by Rankin and Reason (2008) and served as the basis for the survey instrument we created for the current project. In this model, Rankin and Reason posit that campus climate is influenced by six factors: access to higher education and the necessary supports for success and retention; encouragement of diversity in educational and scholarly activities; a diverse student body with educationally purposeful interventions and interactions; diversity education and proactive educational interventions; a university commitment to diversity and social justice through policies addressing harassment and discrimination; and acknowledgment of (and responses to) the influence of society and government. Although these factors are interconnected, they also work independently. The factors' independence, as well as the rich relationships they form, inevitably affect the learning and social outcomes of students in addition to the personal and professional development of faculty, administrators, and staff.

Learning, social, and professional outcomes that are positive for students and employees result when higher education administrators design initiatives that create inclusive campus climates and quality interactive experiences (Rankin & Reason 2005). So that colleges and universities might strengthen their efforts in these areas, research has assessed the experiences of members of majority and minority groups on campus (Malaney et al. 1997; Worthington et al. 2008). Results from two decades of research have shown that historically advantaged groups (e.g., white people, men, and heterosexual people) express more positive views of the campus climate than do such historically disadvantaged groups as members of racial and ethnic minority groups, women, and LGBT individuals (Brown, Clarke, Gortmaker, & Robinson-Keilig 2004; Norris 1992; Rankin & Reason 2005; Worthington et al. 2008).

CAMPUS CLIMATE AND PERSONAL, EDUCATIONAL, AND PROFESSIONAL SUCCESS

Individual perceptions of discrimination or a negative campus climate for intergroup relations can affect student educational outcomes. Sylvia Hurtado and Luis Ponjuan (2005) note that, when stereotypes "pervade the learning environment for minority students[,] . . . student academic performance can be undermined" (236). The literature also suggests that students of color who perceive their campus environment as hostile have higher rates of attrition and have problems adjusting to campus life (Guiffrida, Gouveia, Wall, & Seward 2008; Hurtado & Ponjuan 2005). Students educated at colleges and universities with more inclusive campus environments report feeling more equipped to participate in an increasingly multicultural society (Gurin, Dey, Hurtado, & Gurin 2002). When the campus climate is more positive and students can interact with diverse peers, positive learning occurs and democratic skills are developed (Hurtado & Ponjuan 2005). Racial and ethnic diversity in the campus environment, when coupled with the institution's efforts to foster opportunities for quality interactions and learning from each other, promote "active thinking and personal development" (Gurin et al. 2002:338).

The personal and professional development of faculty, administrators, and staff are also affected by the campus climate. For example, Settles, Cortina, Malley, and Stewart (2006) find that sexual harassment and gender discrimination have a significantly negative impact on the overall attitudes of women faculty toward employment in the academic sciences. A review study by James Sears and Walter Williams (1997) shows that LGB faculty members who judge their campus climate more positively are more likely to feel personally supported and to perceive their work unit as more supportive of hiring and promoting LGB faculty members than do those who view their campus climate more negatively.

The influence of campus climate on employee satisfaction and subsequent productivity is further substantiated by research demonstrating that workplace discrimination and prejudice lead not only to lower health and well-being (i.e., anxiety, depression, and lower life satisfaction and physical health) but also to greater occupational dysfunction (i.e., withdrawal from the organization and lower satisfaction with work, coworkers, and supervisors) (see Silverschanz, Cortina, Konik, & Magley 2008; Waldo 1998).

THE CAMPUS CLIMATE FOR LGBT PEOPLE

Although the number of studies has been limited, research over the past two decades suggests that academe is unwelcoming to LGBT students, faculty, and staff. In a national study of campus climate for underrepresented groups that involved more than 17,000 participants (Rankin 2001), respondents indicated that—of all the underrepresented groups on campus—the climate was "least accepting" of LGBT people, especially transgender people. Forty-two percent of the lesbian, gay, and bisexual (LGB) respondents indicated that they were the targets of harassment based on their sexual orientation; in comparison, 30 percent of the respondents of color reported harassment based on their race and 28 percent of the female respondents reported harassment based on their gender.

Although conditions have improved somewhat over the years for LGBT faculty, students, and staff, Rankin (2003) concludes that they still encounter a hostile climate at most colleges and universities, even on campuses with strong support systems and campus centers for LGBT people. Among the 1,669 self-identified LGBT students, faculty, and administrators surveyed nationwide, 36 percent of the undergraduates and 29 percent of all respondents had experienced harassment over the past year. Ninety-two percent (68) of the transgender respondents reported that they were the targets of harassment because of their gender identity.

Rankin also found that one in five respondents feared for their personal safety on campus because of their sexual and/or gender identities and that half concealed their sexual and/or gender identities to avoid intimidation. Additionally, 41 percent believed that their institutions were not adequately addressing issues related to sexual and gender identity and 43 percent felt that their college or university curricula did not adequately represent the contributions of LGBT people.

In response to these negative campus experiences of LGBT individuals, many colleges and universities have implemented structural changes (Rankin 2003). Typically, the individuals who sought and initiated changes were LGBT faculty, staff, and students and their heterosexual and cisgender allies. Such changes include forming committees charged with the task of improving the quality of life for LGBT students and employees; creating LGBT resource centers and "safe space" programs; offering at least one course on LGBT topics; developing a formal academic program in LGBT studies; providing domestic partner health benefits; establishing LGBT-themed residential programs; including the experiences of LGBT people in student and staff orientations; and instituting nondiscrimination policies that incorporate sexual orientation and gender identity. The findings of Sears and Williams (1997) underscore the positive outcomes of implementing such structural changes. The faculty respondents in their study who work at a college or university that has *not* made changes of this type are less likely to perceive their campus climate as positive than are those who work where a nondiscrimination statement that includes sexual orientation had been enacted, where courses in LGBT studies are offered, or where same-sex partner benefits are available.

Despite the beneficial outcomes of having LGBT-inclusive policies and programs, relatively few institutions have implemented these changes. Currently, 595 colleges and universities offer protection against discrimination on the basis of sexual identity (Human Rights Campaign 2011c), with 392 of these schools enjoining discrimination also on the basis of gender identity (Transgender Law and Policy Institute 2011b). More than 400 institutions provide health care benefits to the same-sex partners of employees (Human Rights Campaign 2011a). These numbers may seem large, but the LGBT-inclusive campuses account for only a small percentage of accredited colleges and universities in the United States. As a result, many LGBT students, staff, and faculty continue to experience the campus climate as hostile and isolating and are frequently victims of discrimination and harassment (Evans & Broido 1999; Tomlinson & Fassinger 2003; Wolf-Wendel, Toma, & Morphew 2001). In fact, physical and verbal harassment of LGBT individuals has been reported on every campus where research has been conducted (Nelson & Krieger 1997).

The national LGBT climate study conducted by Rankin (2003) includes 1,669 LGBT students, faculty, staff, and administrators from fourteen institutions. Twenty-nine percent of all respondents reported experiencing harassment within the last year, with students being the most likely group. Derogatory remarks were the most common form of harassment. Twenty percent of all respondents feared for their personal safety because of their sexual orientation or gender identity, and 51 percent concealed their sexual orientation or gender identity to avoid intimidation. A greater proportion of transgender than of cisgender respondents reported experiences of being harassed. The majority reported that transgender people were the group most likely to be harassed on campus, followed by gay men and then lesbians. Finally, 41 percent of the respondents described their college or university as not thoroughly addressing issues related to sexual orientation and gender identity.

Students are coming out as transgender on college campuses across the country (Beemyn, Curtis, Davis, & Tubbs 2005). Although these students have unique needs related to programming, housing, bathrooms and locker rooms, physical and mental health care, and records and documents, most colleges and universities offer little or no support for this growing population (Beemyn, Curtis, et al. 2005). Rob Pusch (2005) asserts that many transgender students experience isolation and rejection from their family and friends. Unfortunately, such reactions not only are typical of the students' immediate social network but also extend to interactions with other campus community members.

THE IMPACT OF A NEGATIVE CLIMATE

According to Sylvia Hurtado and Deborah Carter (1997), involvement, engagement, and affiliation are central to students' development and progress in college. Furthermore, students' educational success is strongly influenced by the "context of and attitude toward their education . . . including their sense of school and social 'inclusion' and 'exclusion'" (Silverschanz et al. 2008:181). Because "development associated with the college years has far-reaching implications for students' lives," it is imperative that barriers to personal development be addressed for LGBT college students (Hogan & Rentz 1996:310).

Faculty and staff are also affected by the campus environment: an inclusive and welcoming climate helps foster positive job and career attitudes, and a negative climate does just the opposite (Silverschanz et al. 2008). In their study of 768 LGBT workers, Belle Ragins and John Cornwell (2001) explore employees' perceptions and reports of experienced and observed workplace discrimination. They find that LGBT employees are much more likely to *report* anti-LGBT discrimination in organizations that offer same-sex domestic partner benefits and that have nondiscrimination policies and diversity statements that include sexual identity. Also, LGBT individuals were more likely to come out if they worked in organizations that have LGBT-inclusive nondiscrimination policies or if they had LGBT coworkers.

At the same time, perceived workplace discrimination is associated with more negative work attitudes and fewer promotions. The findings of Ragins and Cornwell (2001) suggest that supportive organizational policies have a direct and positive impact on compensation, turnover rate, and organizational and career commitment. In general, organizations that advocated for LGBT individuals had LGBT employees with more positive work attitudes than organizations that failed to do so.

Guided by minority stress theory, Craig Waldo (1998) examines the antecedents and outcomes of heterosexism in the workplace for 287 LGBT employees. His findings indicate that heterosexism is related to higher levels of psychological distress, health-related problems, and decreased satisfaction with multiple aspects of the job. Such outcomes were, in turn, associated with stronger desires to leave or resign from a job and poorer physical and mental health. Moreover, poorer health was related to higher absenteeism and other work-related withdrawal behaviors. These findings are especially disturbing because discriminatory experiences in the workplace not only cause dissatisfaction with work but also affect individuals' overall well-being and their relationships away from the job.

The cited studies on the campus climate for LGBT youth and the workplace climate for LGBT employees underscore the prejudices and discrimination experienced by LGBT individuals. Although the field of education is supposedly bound by ethical principles that require schools to serve the needs of all students, many schools have not yet laid the groundwork necessary to provide educational and social services to LGBT people. The educational outcomes of students are affected by how they experience the campus climate (Rankin & Reason 2005), and the personal and professional development of employees is likewise influenced by their perceptions of and experiences within the workplace climate. Those LGBT employees who judge their workplace climate more positively are more likely to feel personally supported, to perceive their work unit as being more LGBT-inclusive, and to feel that their employer would not disapprove of their "coming out."

In analyzing a transgender community's experiences, Darryl Hill (2002) suggests that three key constructs can be used to conceptualize animosity toward people who are transgender: genderism, transphobia, and gender bashing. *Genderism* is the ideology that there are, and should be, only two genders and that all or most aspects of one's gender are inevitably tied to the gender assigned at birth. Genderism reinforces negative attitudes toward gender nonconformity, or the incongruence between assigned gender and gender identity/expression. Much like heterosexism, genderism is a source of both social oppression and psychological shame; it can be imposed on a person, and a person may internalize that ideology (Lev 2004). *Transphobia* or gender prejudice is the irrational fear, hatred, and/or discriminatory treatment of people whose actual or perceived gender identity/expression does not conform to society's expectations. *Gender bashing* refers to the assault and/or harassment of individuals who are transgender (Wilchins 1997). In short, genderism is the negative cultural ideology, gender prejudice is the emotional expression of that ideology, and gender bashing is the violent manifestation of those emotions (Hill 2002).

Anti-transgender bias is, in part, a logical outgrowth of the genderism prevalent in educational, religious, and governmental institutions. As demonstrated by the research on college campuses, this negative climate fosters hate crimes against transgender people and contributes to their "invisibility." Genderism and gender prejudice may also present transgender victims of hate crimes with special psychological challenges, such as intensified self-hatred, higher levels of depression and anxiety, a loss of confidence, and a heightened sense of vulnerability (Harry 1990; Janoff-Bulman & Frieze 1983; Norris & Kaniasty 1991). Negative feelings regarding the transgender community as well as fear of gender expression and gender identity have been positively correlated with symptoms of psychological depression, and "fear of one's transgender identity" is the strongest predictor for psychological distress (Sánchez & Vilain 2009). The proportion of transgender youth who attempted suicide in 2006 was 20 percent higher than LGB youth and almost five times higher than the U.S. average for all youth (Grossman & D'Augelli 2007). With Hill's (2002) framework for characterizing anti-transgender hatred as a starting point, the current project attempts to provide a more comprehensive view of the climate for transgender people than past studies. Much of the previous research on discrimination, harassment, and violence against transgender people has been based on limited sample sizes, limited reporting, and/or limited geographical locations. Our goal with this project was to rectify these weaknesses by recruiting a large sample of transgender people from across the country.

HOSTILE ENVIRONMENTS

We live in times more sensitive than ever to hatred based violence, especially since the events of September 11th. Yet even now, the deaths of those based on anti-transgender hatred or prejudice are largely ignored. Over the last decade, more than one person per month has died due to transgender-based hate or prejudice, regardless of any other factors in their lives. This trend shows no sign of abating.

—GWENDOLYN ANN SMITH (2000)

From verbal harassment to threats of violence, from acts of discrimination to the destruction of property, from assaults to even murder—people who are (or who are perceived as) transgender often face a hostile social climate. Violent behavior and hostility is an estimated four times higher for transgender individuals when compared with the national average (Koken, Bambi, & Parson 2009; NCAVP 2008). Transgender people are more likely to experience hostile or aggressive familial interaction, more likely to be kicked out of their homes by parents, more likely to become homeless or live below the poverty line, and less likely to be employed (Gehi & Arkles 2007; Koken et al. 2009; Xavier 2006). These compounding factors are likely to result in limited health care access, familial aid, and other resources, and to increase the risk of harassment, discrimination, and violence (Stotzer 2009).

Some of the participants in the current project who are readily seen by others as transgender or gender nonconforming indicated that they cannot even walk down the street or enter a store without being stared at, ridiculed, or threatened with physical assault. Yet other than the few works just cited, little research has been conducted on the prevalence of different forms of anti-transgender harassment and violence. Hate crimes[3] against transgender people were not recognized by the federal government until passage in 2009 of the Matthew Shepard and James Byrd, Jr. Hate Crimes Prevention Act. This act required the Federal Bureau of Investigation to track statistics on hate crimes based on gender identity/expression and gave the Department of Justice the power to investigate and prosecute cases of anti-transgender violence. However, most states still do not recognize transgender people in their hate crime and antidiscrimination laws. Only twelve states and the District of Columbia currently include crimes based on gender identity/expression in hate crime laws, and only fifteen states and the District of Columbia have laws to protect people from discrimination based on their gender identity/expression (National Gay and Lesbian Task Force 2011a, 2011b).

Some data about transgender-related hate crimes are collected by advocacy and social service groups, most notably the National Coalition of Anti-Violence Programs (NCAVP). According to its most recent report on LGBT violence (NCAVP 2008), 288 (16 percent) of the incidents reviewed by the group in the preceding year were motivated in whole or in part by anti-transgender bias. However, the report covered only a limited number of U.S. states and cities, and these areas recorded relatively few anti-transgender crimes. As with other types of bias-motivated crime, it is likely that violence against transgender people is vastly underreported (GenderPAC 2006).

The reluctance of transgender people to report harassment and violence indicates the extent of discrimination and stigma against individuals who are perceived as gender different; it also reflects a lack of knowledge and understanding of transgender issues by law enforcement officials and by some social and public service organizations. In a national survey of 402 transgender people, Lombardi et al. (2001) find that 60 percent of the respondents had experienced some type of violence or harassment related to gender identity. In terms of the types of offenses they reported, 56 percent had been harassed or verbally abused, 30 percent had been assaulted with or without a weapon, 17 percent had objects thrown at them, 14 percent had been robbed, and 8 percent experienced what they considered to be an unjustified arrest. The researchers conclude that, among the transgender participants, "older people, those employed full-time, and those with a high income all have lower probability of experiencing violence" (97).

The lack of prosecution for crimes motivated by anti-transgender bias—and the lack of respect typically accorded to transgender people who do report crimes—are evidence that the judicial system fails to take seriously violence against transgender people (Daley, Kulger, & Hirshman 2000; GenderPAC 1997; Moran & Sharpe 2001, 2004). In a study by GenderPAC (2006) examining the murders of transgender youth from 1995 to 2005, the homicides classified as hate crimes were about one-and-a-half times more likely (50 versus 33 percent) to result in the apprehension of a suspect than those that were not so classified. Almost three-quarters of the attacks against transgender individuals were not classified as hate crimes, often despite clear evidence to the contrary. Moreover, only 46 percent of the murders identified in the GenderPAC report have been solved to date. This compares with a 69 percent resolution rate for all homicides nationally.[4]

In addition to these national reports and studies, several community surveys have also attempted to measure the prevalence of violence directed toward transgender people (Clements-Nolle, Marx, & Katz 2006; Kenagy 2005; Risser, Shelton, McCurdy, Atkinson, Padgett, & Useche 2005; Stotzer 2008; Xavier, Bobbin, Singer, & Budd 2005). The results of these surveys suggest that people who are transgender experience high rates of verbal and physical harassment because of their gender identity/expression. For example, in a needs assessment of 248 transgender individuals in Washington, DC, most of whom were people of color, Xavier et al. (2005) find that 43 percent of the participants had been victims of violence. This figure includes the 13 percent who reported being sexually assaulted or raped.

Kim Felsenthal (2004) suggests that attacks on people who are transgender are based on a desire to keep the binary gender system in place. In response to this victimization, some transgender people revert to societal gender expectations in order to avoid further intimidation. Tarynn Witten and Evan Eyler (1999) argue that anti-transgender hate crimes are often characterized as being committed by male "predators" or as being provoked by the victims themselves—by violating gender norms or failing to disclose their transgender identity up front. The authors see both of these explanations as "simply extensions of the traditional discourse regarding violence against women: either the perpetrator is a 'mad dog' (i.e., a criminally deviant male) or the victim 'asked for it' (via exhibiting the 'provocative behavior' of failing to conform to gender role expectations)" (461).

However, examining the details of hate crimes against transgender people indicates that far more than just the management of gender norms is involved. Rebecca Stotzer (2008) suggests that people who are transgender are "rarely attacked solely because of their gender identity" but rather are typically targeted because of the intersection of different identities (50). Similarly, Leslie Moran and Andrew Sharpe (2004) contend that the multiple and simultaneous operation of many different cultural and social identities complicate our understanding of bias crimes against transgender people. The GenderPAC (2006) study supports this premise in that "youth of color account for 91 percent of victims for which race is known, with Black and Latino victims accounting for the vast majority (85 percent)" (4). This finding suggests that the intersection of racism and genderism may increase bias crimes against transgender people of color.

In order to assess the extent to which aspects of identity other than gender identity/expression affect anti-transgender harassment as well as how this harassment is experienced, we shall also consider age, sexual orientation, level of outness, and race as possible factors in individuals being harassed, fearing for their physical safety, concealing their transgender identity to avoid intimidation, and being denied employment or promotion. The following sections discuss the harassment and discrimination reported by the participants in our survey.

Twenty-seven percent (955) of the survey respondents indicated that they had been harassed within the past year because of their gender identity and/or gender expression. When reviewing the data by transgender group, 47 percent (49) of the female-to-different-gender participants experienced harassment as compared to 22 percent (33) of the male-to-different-gender participants, 27 percent (584) of the male-to-female/transgender participants, and 35 percent (231) of the female-to-male/transgender participants. The confounding variable of age accounts for the higher percentage of FTDG people who reported being harassed, as nearly three-fourths of these respondents were less than twenty-three years old—the youngest average age among the transgender groups—and the younger people we surveyed experienced harassment more commonly.

Age. Participants who were less than nineteen years old and nineteen to twenty-two years old at the time of the survey were more likely (44 and 38 percent, respectively) than participants in other age groups to indicate that they had been harassed in the past year because of their gender identity/expression. Although it happened a few years before, one of the most horrific incidents was recounted by Caiden, a twenty-one-year-old interviewee who self-identifies as transgender. Soon after finishing high school, when ze was working at a video rental store and presenting as masculine, Caiden was attacked by three of hir former classmates, who recognized hir as transgender and were waiting for hir when hir shift ended. Ze was beaten with a piece of wood and sexually assaulted before ze lost consciousness. Caiden never reported the crime, because ze was not out at the time and did not want hir parents to know about hir gender identity.

Participants who were at least fifty-three years old experienced the least amount of harassment (11 percent) because, in part, they were the age group most likely to be completely closeted to friends, colleagues, and family members. Ageism may also play a part, since older people are often ignored in modern society or seen as non-threatening. One of the oldest participants, Pat, transitioned in his late sixties. Now seventy-three years old, he has not encountered harassment or violence despite being very open about being a transsexual man.

Sexual Orientation. The individuals who indicated "other" as their sexual orientation were most likely to experience harassment (41 percent, 230 people), followed by gay people (31 percent, 40), asexual people (29 percent, 52), lesbian (28 percent, 118) and bisexual people (28 percent, 318), and heterosexual people (19 percent, 196). Among the identities of the "other" respondents were "homo-flexible," "bicurious," "bisexual when dressed as a woman, heterosexual when dressed as a man," "don't know," "heterosexual lesbian," "lesbian with bisexual leanings," "omnisexual," "pansexual," and "queer." Our finding that heterosexual individuals were the least likely to report being harassed confirms the results of a previous study involving campus populations (Rankin 2003), which found that the transgender college students, staff, and faculty who identified as heterosexual were the least likely to indicate experiencing harassment.

Level of Outness. Some transgender people have no choice about whether to disclose their gender identity. If they are transitioning where they live and work, or if others perceive them as presenting as a gender different from their assigned gender, then they are out by default and often subject to harassment and discrimination. In our survey, the more the participants were known as transgender, the greater their risk for harassment. Respondents who reported that they were out to all of their friends were the most likely to state that they had experienced anti-transgender harassment within the last year (40 percent, 383 people), whereas those who reported they were completely closeted were the least likely to state that they had experienced such harassment (10 percent, 52 people). Similarly, respondents who indicated that they were entirely or mostly out to their nuclear families, extended families, and colleagues were more likely to report harassment because of their gender identity/ expression than the individuals who were totally closeted or were out to only a few members of each group.

Race. Among the individuals surveyed, a significantly larger percentage of transgender people of color (33 percent) reported experiencing harassment in the previous year because of their gender identity/expression than did transgender white people (27 percent). This difference demonstrates how racism and genderism can intersect in the lives of transgender people of color. Examining the data by specific racial categories, 43 percent of the American Indian respondents (66 people), 32 percent of the Latino(a)/Hispanic/ Chicano(a) respondents (41 people), 29 percent of the African/ African American/black respondents (23 people), and 27 percent of the Asian/Asian American respondents (24 people) reported experiencing harassment.

HOW RESPONDENTS EXPERIENCED HARASSMENT AND VIOLENCE

The most common forms of harassment reported across age, sexual orientation, and racial groups were derogatory remarks (24 percent, 838 people) and direct or indirect verbal harassment/threats (16 percent, 574 people). Other frequent responses included pressure to be silent about being transgender (10 percent, 333), threats of physical violence (7 percent, 252), denial of services (7 percent, 245), and threats to expose their gender identity (6 percent, 210). Eighty participants (2 percent) indicated that they had been physically assaulted.

A significantly higher incidence of physical assault was reported by transgender people of color than by transgender white respondents. Specifically, a significantly greater percentage of the respondents who identified their racial identity as African/African American/ black, Asian/Asian American, Latino(a)/Hispanic/Chicano(a), and/ or American Indian than of white respondents (17 versus 7 percent) reported that they had been physically assaulted. Thus, the combination of racism and genderism may account for the greater rate of physical assaults among transgender people of color.

One of the participants, Andy, a twenty-one-year-old Asian American transgender woman, was harassed and punched in the face by a group of unknown young men as she was walking home from work in 2006. Adding to her victimization, the police never responded when she called to report the assault. As in Andy's case, the most common location where harassment occurred was in a public space (72 percent, 692 people). Some of the public areas mentioned were clothing stores, parking lots, airports, medical centers, college campuses, high schools, and online chat rooms. Other sites of harassment were the workplace (9 percent, 319) and, notably, at LGBT events (3 percent, 97)—demonstrating that even locations that are supposed to be inclusive and supportive of transgender people are not always safe spaces.

Andy's experience was typical also in that the most common source of harassment was people whom the participants did not know (8 percent, 285 individuals), followed by colleagues or co-workers (7 percent, 258), family members (6 percent, 203), and supervisors/managers/bosses (5 percent, 158). Twenty-five individuals (3 percent) identified the police as the perpetrators; this is especially noteworthy since, as other research (Moran & Sharpe 2004) has found, transgender people often do not report hate crimes because they have been or fear being harassed by law enforcement officials. The largest number of participants (13 percent, 470 people) indicated some "other" source for the harassment. These responses included "teacher," "manager at store," "acquaintance," "children," "church member," "client," "fellow students," "friend," "insurance company," and "neighbor."

Asked how they responded to the harassment, a majority of the participants indicated that they did nothing that would lead to the harasser being identified or prosecuted. The most common reaction to the harassment was feeling embarrassed (13 percent, 460 people), followed by telling a friend (12 percent, 412), avoiding the harasser (11 percent, 393), leaving the situation immediately (11 percent, 368), and ignoring the harassment (10 percent, 339). Fewer than 10 percent of respondents confronted the harasser at the time (or sometime later), and only 6 percent lodged a complaint with the appropriate authority.

The prevalence of harassment and violence against transgender people contributed to a climate of fear among many of the participants, a majority of whom indicated that they sometimes or often feared for their physical safety because of their gender identity/expression. Fourteen percent of each transgender group reported that they often felt unsafe. However, the FTM/transgender and female-to-different-gender respondents were slightly more likely than the MTF/transgender and male-to-different-gender respondents to report that they sometimes felt unsafe (respectively 44 and 52 percent versus 38 and 37 percent). The degree to which the participants feared for their physical safety varied more extensively by age, sexual orientation, level of outness, and race.

Age. In general, the younger the individual surveyed, the greater the likelihood that the person felt unsafe because of his/her/hir gender identity/expression. Nineteen percent of the participants who were eighteen years old or less and 18 percent of those who were nineteen to twenty-two years old reported that they often feared for their physical safety, as compared with just 6 percent of respondents who were at least fifty-three years old. At the other extreme, 30 percent of the fifty-three-and-older participants stated that they never felt unsafe—more than twice the percentage of the two youngest age groups. As mentioned previously, the older respondents were less likely to be out and to have experienced harassment than members of other age groups, so they were not as fearful for their safety.

Sexual Orientation. The lesbian, gay, bisexual, and asexual respondents were more likely than the heterosexual respondents to indicate that they sometimes or often felt unsafe (52–61 versus 41 percent). The individuals who identified as heterosexual also had a higher rate of never fearing for their physical safety. Transgender participants who met sociocultural expectations (i.e., were attracted to people of a different gender) were less likely to have experienced harassment, and this probably contributed to their being less likely to fear for their physical safety.

Level of Outness. Many of the participants—regardless of their level of outness to friends, immediate family, extended family, and colleagues—reported that they feared for their physical safety because of their gender identity/expression. A majority (55–58 percent) of those who were out to several, most, or all of their friends indicated feeling sometimes or often unsafe. Not surprisingly, the respondents who were totally closeted (28 percent, 150 people) or were out to only a few friends (23 percent, 193 people) were more likely than the other groups to report that they never feared for their physical safety.

Our findings are similar with regard to participants' outness to their nuclear families, extended families, and colleagues. A majority of those who were more out to these groups sometimes or often feared for their physical safety. Yet many of the individuals who were out to only a few extended family members or colleagues also felt unsafe, sometimes or often, perhaps reflecting a concern that people whom they knew less well would be more likely to react violently or to inform others who might respond negatively. As with the level of outness to friends, participants who were totally closeted to family and colleagues were more likely than participants who were at least partially out to report that they never felt unsafe.

Race. The transgender people of color whom we surveyed were significantly more afraid for their safety than were the transgender white people. Breaking down the data for people of color by specific racial groups, 73 percent of the African/African American/black respondents, 70 percent of the Asian/Asian American respondents, 82 percent of the Latino(a)/Hispanic/Chicano(a) respondents, and 87 percent of the American Indian respondents reported that they feared for their physical safety. Given that almost all of the transgender participants of color had been physically assaulted, this fear was well founded.

CONCEALING ONE'S IDENTITY TO AVOID INTIMIDATION

Given that many transgender people experience and/or fear experiencing harassment and violence, we asked the extent to which the participants intentionally concealed their gender identity to avoid intimidation. A majority of all of the individuals surveyed reported that they sometimes or often hid their transgender identity, with the MTF/transgender and male-to-different-gender respondents more likely to report that they *often* did so and the FTM/transgender and female-to-different-gender respondents more likely to report that they *sometimes* did so.

Age. Many participants (39–48 percent) of all ages stated that they often concealed their gender identity to avoid intimidation. Much fewer (11–15 percent) indicated that they never did so. The one exception were the respondents who were at least fifty-three years old; 23 percent of this group reported that they never concealed their gender identity. The reason for this difference may be that a number of the older respondents, some of whom had transitioned many years before or had been cross-dressing since they were young, were comfortable with themselves and felt secure in their lives. They were not concerned if others found out, and some were open about their gender identity in order to educate others. Maggie, a fifty-three-year-old interviewee, states: "I'm fairly well known as a TS [transsexual] person, both at work and in my community. I feel no need to hide what I am. The only way the world will eventually stop rejecting TS people is for the majority to meet us and understand that, in most instances, we are simply ordinary, well-meaning people."

Sexual Orientation. A majority of people (67–71 percent) of all sexual orientations reported that they sometimes or often concealed their gender identity to avoid discrimination. The heterosexual participants were just as likely as the lesbian, gay, and bisexual participants to eschew disclosure. There was also not any statistical difference between the heterosexual and the lesbian, gay, and bisexual respondents who never sought to hide their transgender identity: roughly equal percentages (ranging from 12 to 15 percent) of people of all sexual orientations indicated that they never concealed their gender identity.

Race. As with sexual orientation, there were no significant differences by race with regard to concealing one's transgender identity. The transgender people of color surveyed did not conceal their gender identity more or less frequently than the transgender white people.

DENIED EMPLOYMENT OR PROMOTION

To determine if the atmosphere for transgender workers has changed in the last twenty years, Berry, McGuffee, Rush, and Columbus (2003) compare the benchmark case of Audra Sommers, a transsexual woman who was fired from her job in 1980, to more recent cases of anti-transgender discrimination. The authors conclude that employment discrimination remains evident, but they argue that the workplace climate is improving for some transgender people and that courts increasingly rule in favor of transgender worker rights. Nonetheless, acceptance in the workplace remains an unfulfilled dream for most transgender people, especially for individuals who are transitioning on the job. In the NGLTF/NCTE (2009) survey of 6,450 transgender and gender-nonconforming people, 97 percent of respondents reported experiencing harassment or discrimination in the workplace. Instances of mistreatment described by the respondents included removal from direct contact with clients, disclosure of confidential information to coworkers, loss of employment, and physical or sexual assault.

We asked the participants in our survey if they had ever been denied employment, advancement, or a raise because of their gender identity/expression. We find that there are no significant differences in reported workplace discrimination among the MTF/T, MTDG, FTM/T, and FTDG respondents. About half (44–52 percent) of the participants in each group indicated that, to their knowledge, they have never been denied employment or a promotion because of their gender identity/expression; at the other extreme, 8 to 11 percent stated that they have often encountered workplace bias. It is difficult to be certain that one's transgender identity affected a hiring or promotion decision, and accordingly one-fifth to one-quarter of each group reported that they did not know if they had experienced employment discrimination.

The interviewees shared a wide range of workplace experiences. Diana C. transitioned from male to female while continuing to work at the police department where she has served as an officer for twenty-five years. "Most people have responded very professionally," she relates. "A few are obviously uncomfortable with the situation, but I haven't experienced anything that I would call harassment or employment discrimination." Another MTF participant, Lea, who works on a military base, also reported a positive transition experience.

All 200+ of my coworkers were told by name that I was going to [be] coming back to work in January [2004] as a woman and that management was supporting my life decision. Everyone was told that if they had religious/moral challenges to leave them in their cars when they got to work and that acts of discrimination against me would not be tolerated. . . . This year, only one individual was counseled for discrimination for defamatory statements [that] a supervisor overheard him saying to a coworker. In fact, the working relationships with my coworkers have improved because I seem "less uptight" and happy. . . . The acceptance by my coworkers has been quicker and easier than I had anticipated.

Lynn L., a thirty-five-year-old transsexual female interviewee, had the opposite experience. She was fired from two jobs when she told her supervisors that she would be transitioning, and she has not been able to find work since then. Because she is unemployed, Lynn does not have health insurance and thus can no longer afford hormones. She faces a dilemma: she encounters anti-transgender discrimination because she does not look like other women, but without a job she cannot afford to alter her body to look more traditionally female.

Robert, a fifty-one-year-old transsexual man, chose to take his chances finding other work when he experienced employment discrimination. He states: "I walked out on the job I had when I was diagnosed because they would not let me transition at work and I would not put up with one more day of trying to pretend to be female." Kim D., a fifty-one-year-old transsexual female participant, also encountered opposition from her supervisors when she sought to transition at work. But rather than quitting her job as a pharmacist, she filed discrimination charges against her employer. Settling out of court, the company agreed to recognize her as female; she was allowed to dress like other women at work and was asked to advise management regarding any instances of mistreatment from her coworkers. Although Kim is relieved that she did not have to change jobs when she transitioned, she resents being forced to engage in a yearlong battle simply to be treated with respect by her employer.

Interviewees who identified as genderqueer or as another nonbinary gender identity and who presented as androgynous or as different genders at different times faced additional workplace obstacles. Most of these respondents were not fully transitioning and so did not fit into dichotomous gender expectations, which can be more challenging and unsettling to employers and coworkers than individuals who present as strictly female or male. Several of the nonbinary-gendered interviewees were able to avoid potential workplace problems related to their gender identity/expression by being employed in transgender-supportive environments. Examples include Shannon, a genderqueer participant who works for an HIV/AIDS foundation, and "Mar," a bigender interviewee who is known to coworkers as both "Mark" and "Marla" and works in an industry "where you can express social needs."

A review of the respondents' experiences with employment discrimination by their age, sexual orientation, level of outness, and race reveals that only the differences based on race are statistically significant.

Age. Many (45–58 percent) of the respondents across age groups reported that, to their knowledge, they have never been denied employment, advancement, or a raise on account of their gender identity/expression. The individuals who were at least fifty-three years old at the time of the survey were the most likely to state that they have not experienced job discrimination. Some of these older respondents had transitioned many years before and were not known as transgender to the people that they had since met, so they were rarely subjected to anti-transgender bias. Zach, a forty-nine-year-old FTM interviewee, increasingly finds himself in this position. He states: "I was open about [being transgender] for the first two years [after transitioning], [but] then realized I don't have to tell people. I transitioned for me, not to be in people's faces. I seldom make it part of my conversation with folks I meet. At this point over half the people in my life don't know. As I age, I'm sure fewer and fewer people will know." A substantial percentage (17–23 percent) of respondents in each age group indicated that they did not know if they had encountered workplace bias, whereas much fewer (6–11 percent) indicated that they have often experienced it.

Sexual Orientation. The heterosexual respondents were more likely (56 versus 41–50 percent) than the lesbian, gay, bisexual, and asexual (LGBA) respondents to indicate that, to their knowledge, they had never been denied employment, advancement, or a raise because of their gender identity/expression. At the same time, a higher percentage (18–28 versus 13 percent) of the LGBA individuals than the heterosexual individuals surveyed reported that they sometimes or often experienced workplace discrimination. About one-fourth to one-fifth of participants across sexual orientation categories stated that they did not know whether they had ever been denied a job or a promotion because of anti-transgender bias.

Level of Outness. Not surprisingly, the participants who stated that they were completely closeted to their colleagues were the most likely (55 percent) to report that they had never been denied employment, advancement, or a raise because of their gender identity/expression. Yet many of the participants (43–49 percent) who were out to varying degrees also indicated that they had never experienced anti-transgender workplace discrimination. Nevertheless, those who stated that they were out to all of their colleagues were the most likely (35 percent) to report sometimes or often being denied employment or promotion, and the totally closeted individuals were the least likely (9 percent). One way that being out can affect a person's job was evident in the experiences of Joann Marie, a white transsexual female participant. She stated: "Discussing transition[ing] on the job resulted, initially, in the company asking me to delay while employees were readied for the change, but after I was televised testifying at a public hearing in favor of a local human rights law, they fired me." The discrimination she faced demonstrated the need for the law, as she had no recourse following her dismissal.

Race. As with other forms of harassment, workplace discrimination was more likely to be reported by participants who are people of color than by white participants. Twenty-five percent of the surveyed people of color stated that they had sometimes or often been denied employment, advancement, or a raise, as compared with 16 percent of the white respondents. Breaking down the data for people of color by specific racial groups, 33 percent of the African/African American/black respondents, 28 percent of the Asian/Asian American respondents, 35 percent of the Latino(a)/Hispanic/Chicano(a) respondents, and 46 percent of the American Indian respondents reported that they had been denied employment, advancement, or a raise. Again, the intersection of racial and anti-transgender bias seems to increase the likelihood of discrimination.

The interviewee comments suggest that the biggest factor in employment discrimination for many participants was their particular circumstances—the job they held, the culture of the workplace, their relationships with coworkers, the attitudes of senior managers, and the laws of the city and state. As demonstrated by Lea's and Diana's experiences, even places that are typically thought of as unfriendly to transgender people (e.g., police departments and military bases) can be supportive environments if coworkers are willing to be open-minded and if institutional leaders clearly and forcefully indicate that they will not tolerate anti-transgender harassment. That being said, a number of interviewees received scant support from management or colleagues and thus, like Lynn L., lost their jobs or, like Robert, were forced to quit.

SUMMARY OF THE CLIMATE FOR TRANSGENDER PEOPLE

Clearly, harassment and discrimination continue to be a concern for many transgender people. Despite the growing number of states, municipalities, colleges, and corporations that have added "gender identity/expression" to their nondiscrimination laws and policies (Human Rights Campaign 2011b; National Gay and Lesbian Task Force 2010; Transgender Law and Policy Institute 2011b), more than a fourth of the respondents to our survey indicated that they had experienced harassment in the past year. Moreover, 19 percent have sometimes or often been denied employment or advancement because of their gender identity/expression. Many other participants sometimes or often concealed their gender identity in an attempt to avoid mistreatment.

Despite greater societal recognition of transgender people and a growing transgender rights movement, individuals who are (or are perceived as) transgender commonly continue to face discrimination, harassment, and bias-motivated violence in many areas of their lives. These conditions mean that many transgender people are unemployed or underemployed and, as a result, face a constant struggle for economic security. As documented in this chapter, workplace discrimination and prejudice lead to negative job and career attitudes, lower satisfaction with coworkers and supervisors, greater anxiety and depression, and poorer physical health. The widespread adoption of transgender-inclusive workplace nondiscrimination policies and practices would provide a crucial foundation for transgender people as a whole to lead healthier, more dignified, and more economically secure lives.

Maggie

Janet

Michael with his mother and brother

Mark and his wife, Violet

DEVELOPMENTAL MILESTONES OF DIFFERENT TRANSGENDER GROUPS

I went through the labels . . . tomboy in childhood, dyke in my life after divorce from a man, butch in middle-age, then trans as I became aware of it.

—EUGENE

I have identified with everything from male, CD, transgender in the old sense of the word, transsexual, to now a marginally female person that happens to be a transsexual. . . . Being a transsexual was not exactly a first choice. I tried other identities and all of them would have been preferable to being a transsexual. However, you can only deny the truth for so long.

— "MELANIE"

We developed the survey that serves as the basis for this book because we recognized the need for more and better data on the processes through which people begin to identify as transgender. We also conducted this work because we wanted to offer a more inclusive and more nuanced look at the lives of transgender people. Previous research has often treated transgender people as a single, unified group—frequently in the context of research on LGBT people—or has focused on one segment of transgender communities (e.g., cross-dressing men or transsexual women). Our work sought to address the experiences of a wide range of gender-different people, including individuals who describe themselves as female-to-male transsexuals (FTMs), transsexual men, and men with transsexual pasts; male-to-female transsexuals (MTFs), transsexual women, and women with transsexual pasts; cross-dressers (CDs) and t-girls; and genderqueers, third genders, androgynes, and others with nonbinary gender identities.

As this partial list of gender-different identities and expressions demonstrates, people whose genders are generally considered to fall under the "transgender" umbrella think of and name themselves in myriad ways. Even transgender people who seemingly share a similar life history can have very different understandings of their identities. For example, female-assigned individuals of approximately the same age, race, and class who identify as and transition to male may identify variously as transgender, as transsexual men, or as simply men. These self-descriptors are often indicative of differences in how they see themselves and live their lives, including the extent to which they present as male and are open to others about their gender history.

Despite these differences, we found through our work that individuals who are transitioning or changing their gender expression from female to male or from male to female, who cross-dress, or who identify and/or express their gender in nonbinary ways often experience similar events in the process of identifying as a member of a transgender group. We refer to these events as *milestones* because they are important life moments for many of the participants. This chapter begins with a review of existing transgender identity development models. We then outline and describe milestones for FTM individuals and transsexual men, for MTF individuals and transsexual women, for female-presenting cross-dressers,[1] and for genderqueer individuals and people with fluid gender identities.

MODELS OF TRANSGENDER IDENTITY DEVELOPMENT

As transgender people have become more visible and more socially organized in the past two decades, a growing number of researchers have examined the development of transgender identities. Most of this research focuses on the experiences of transsexual women and/or men. Anne Bolin (1988) and Frank Lewins (1995) propose models intended to explain the process by which individuals come to identify as transsexual women. Bolin offers a four-stage schema of transsexual "becoming" that considers personal and social identity transformation, phenotypic transformation, and rite of transformation. Individuals move from a state of gender confusion and/or feeling that they are more similar to girls than boys, to having a transsexual primary identity, to having a primary identity as women, and finally to rejecting a transsexual identity and seeing themselves as a "natural woman." As part of this process, they increasingly present as women and feminize their bodies through hormones and surgery.

Lewins suggests a six-stage model that starts with MTF individuals having a sense of "abiding anxiety," because of feeling uncomfortable with their gender assignment. In the second stage, "discovery," they begin to learn about transsexuality and recognize that gender transition is possible; however, they deny that this identity applies to them in the third stage, "purging and delay." After finally accepting themselves as transsexual women (stage four), they pursue "sex reassignment" (stage five) and achieve "invisibility" as individuals who had been assigned male at birth (stage six).

Lewins and Bolin thus both expect that someone who transitions will no longer identify as transgender. Lewins argues that MTF individuals will seek to "disappear" as transsexuals and hide their pasts, which may involve changing jobs, moving to a new city, severing ties whenever possible with old acquaintances, and/or avoiding social contact with other transsexual individuals. Although some do follow this path, many transsexual women and men openly acknowledge their transgender histories today and take pride in this identity, rather than considering it shameful or stigmatizing and seeking to become invisible (Bornstein 1994; Feinberg 1998; Green 2004). They recognize that being transsexual does not make them any less of a woman or man.

Another weakness of the models of Lewins and Bolin is that they have gender reassignment or confirmation surgery as the final and natural outcome of their developmental processes. But as Bolin (1994) states in her subsequent research, more and more transsexual women are choosing not to have surgery even when it is financially and medically possible. Noting the "greater acceptance over the past decade of nonsurgical options for physical males wishing to live as women," she finds that seemingly "there has been a 'coming out of the closet' of those who regard themselves as nonsurgically inclined" (461, 467). The expectation of genital surgery would be even less applicable to FTM individuals, who often experience their lives as men without "bottom" surgery (Cromwell 1999; Rubin 2003).

The assumption of surgery aside, the models that have been proposed to describe the process of transsexual male identity development have much in common with the transsexual female identity models. As in Lewins's schema, the female-assigned people in the first stage of Jeremy Baumbach and Louisa Turner's (1992) three-component model of "female gender disorder" have a feeling of discontent or discomfort with their gender. The individuals may begin to wish that they were male as a "fantasized solution" to their feelings (stage two) and then, as in the MTF identity models, act on this desire by pursuing "sex reassignment" (stage three). However, Baumbach and Turner define reassignment more broadly than do Lewins and Bolin, recognizing that FTM individuals may transition through taking hormones and might not seek or complete all gender confirmation surgeries.

Henry Rubin (2003) uses sociologist Barbara Ponse's (1978) concept of a *trajectory*, a nonsequential path taken in developing an identity, to explain the process by which transsexual men consolidate their identities. He finds that the first four "stops" in Ponse's trajectory—"experiencing a subjective feeling of difference," "finding the appropriate category and assigning the feeling of difference a meaning," "accepting the category as descriptive of one's experience," and "seeking a community"—are useful for describing the experiences of FTM individuals. The first three of these stops roughly correspond to Lewins's stages of "abiding anxiety," "discovery," and "acceptance." Rubin's culminating stop, "making transition choices," also mirrors other transsexual models and acknowledges the different choices that FTM individuals have in deciding how they will present and live their lives as men.

A number of researchers (Devor 1997a, 2004a, 2004b; Ekins 1997; Hogan-Finlay et al. 1997; Lev 2004) have expanded on theories that seek to explain the identity formation processes of transsexual women or men, proposing models that consider cross-gender identity and expression more broadly. Richard Ekins and Mary Hogan-Finlay et al. suggest similar approaches to describe what Ekins (1997:2) calls "male femaling": the social process by which individuals assigned male at birth present as female "in various ways, in various contexts, at various times, with various stagings, and with various consequences." In both models, initial cross-dressing and imagining or wishing that one were female are the first two stages. However, the third stage for Hogan-Finlay et al. is the "public expression of female persona" whereas Ekins proposes a more general stage of "doing female," which may involve regular and public cross-dressing but could also be limited to solitary cross-dressing. Since many individuals who cross-dress are satisfied with doing so in private, Ekins's framework is more inclusive of the range of cross-gender experiences. Another advantage of Ekins's model is that he acknowledges how individuals seek to make sense of their cross-gender identities and find a label that fits in a stage he refers to as "constituting femaling." Ekins and Hogan-Finlay et al. each view the creation of a permanent cross-gender identity as their final stage, but Hogan-Finlay et al. apply this stage only to transsexual individuals and so fail to recognize that many cross-dressing men also develop female identities that are an integral and lasting part of themselves.

Sociologist Aaron Devor proposes a theory for transsexual male and female identity development that draws from Vivienne Cass's (1979) model of homosexual identity formation and incorporates elements from Helen Rose Fuchs Ebaugh's (1988) work on the process of role exit. The six stages of Cass's model—"identity confusion," "identity comparison," "identity tolerance," "identity acceptance," "identity pride," and "identity synthesis"—are also stages in Devor's (2004a, 2004b) model, with Devor including stages of "confusion" and "comparison" about the individual's assigned gender and sex and about transsexual or transgender identities. Like Lewins (1995), Devor also proposes stages of "abiding anxiety" and "delay" before people accept themselves as transgender or transsexual, though Devor adds a second stage of "delay" before an individual decides to transition.

Among his fourteen stages, then, Devor has two stages of "identity confusion" and two stages of "delay," reflecting the struggle that many transgender people have faced in understanding themselves, overcoming denial, and establishing an identity that remains socially stigmatized. Transgender individuals do often encounter personal and societal obstacles in the process of identity formation; however, many younger people indicate that they readily recognized and accepted themselves as transgender. They can now see transgender images in popular culture, read about transgender issues in the mainstream media, and connect with other transgender youth through web pages, chat rooms, social networking sites, and other online venues. As a result, it seems that significantly fewer younger transgender people today lack information for an extended period of time or have a sense of prolonged confusion, which undermines Devor's focus on these experiences.

Arlene Istar Lev, a clinical social worker, also proposes a general model of transsexual identity formation and suggests how therapists can assist transsexual individuals at each of her six "states of emergence." Lev's (2004) model shares some important elements with other theories; among her stages are "awareness," "seeking information/reaching out," finding an "identity and self-labeling," "transition issues," and "acceptance and post-transition issues." But unique among the models discussed here, Lev adds a stage of "disclosure to significant others"—spouses, partners, family members, and friends. This step is a critical one to include, as many transsexual individuals experience great anxiety over when and how to tell other people about their gender identities and, moreover, see disclosure as a major hurdle in the process of becoming their "true selves."

A MILESTONE SCHEMA

Unlike many theories of transgender identity development, our milestone schema is not a stage or step model—even though there is a seemingly "natural" progression through the milestones from confusion, guilt, and shame to self-acceptance and a sense of wholeness. Moreover, not all milestones are relevant to all individuals within a given transgender group, and even people who experience the same milestone will likely do so in different ways. For example, we found that many of the transsexual female participants first thought of themselves as cross-dressers and that many of the transsexual male participants first identified as lesbians; hence we included these events as milestones. Yet a significant number of the respondents did not share these experiences. Some of the transsexual women always felt themselves to be women and never believed that they were cross-dressers, and some of the transsexual men were attracted to other men or were attracted to women but felt this attraction *as men* (that is, they considered themselves to be heterosexual).

Similarly, some of the milestones were less applicable (or not at all) to a number of the younger transgender participants, who grew up with greater access to information and resources than did transgender people in previous decades. Because they learned about and accepted the idea of being transgender at a young age, they did not first identify as some other identity or need to overcome denial. Many of the younger transgender respondents also reached certain milestones sooner, such as knowing about and meeting other transgender people.

Instead of a model, the milestones represent common themes—events often experienced by people in each transgender group in the process of recognizing and acknowledging themselves as gender different. For most participants, this process involved not only accepting themselves psychologically but also changing their appearance physically by, for example, taking hormones, having gender confirmation surgeries, fully cross-dressing, and/or presenting androgynously. It also entailed deciding whether to tell their family and friends about being transgender (if their identity was not obvious from their gender expression) and becoming comfortable with how they look, even if they differ anatomically or in their outward appearance from most other women or men. The milestones for each transgender group are summarized in table 4.1.

TABLE 4.1 Milestones for each gender group

FTM Milestones	MTF Milestones	CD Milestones	GQ Milestones
Feeling and often expressing a male gender identity from a young age	Feeling and often expressing a female gender identity from a young age	Attraction to "women's" clothes and cross-dressing from a young age	Feeling and often expressing a different gender identity from a young age
Repressing or hiding one's male gender identity in the face of hostility and/or isolation	Repressing or hiding one's female gender identity in the face of hostility and/or isolation	Buying or obtaining one's own "women's" clothing	Realizing that genderqueer is a viable identity
Thinking of oneself as lesbian, but realizing over time it was not a good fit	Learning about and meeting other transsexual women	Repressing the desire to cross-dress and purging clothing because of shame	Deciding how to express oneself as genderqueer
Realizing that there are FTM individuals and that transitioning is possible	Recognizing oneself as transsexual, rather than as a cross-dresser	Learning about and meeting other cross-dressers	Encountering resistance to a nonbinary gender expression or identity
Learning about and meeting other transsexual men	Overcoming denial and internalized genderism to accept oneself as female	Overcoming shame to accept oneself as a cross-dresser	Not fitting in with transgender or LGBT communities
Overcoming denial and internalized genderism to accept oneself as male	Taking hormones and perhaps having surgery to look more like self-image	Cross-dressing in public for the first time and adopting a feminine name	Creating a home within or outside of transgender/LGBT communities
Taking hormones and having top surgery to look more like self-image	Whether and when to tell others, and developing new relationships after disclosure	Whether and when to tell others, and developing new relationships after disclosure	
Whether and when to tell others, and developing new relationships after disclosure	Having a sense of wholeness even when unable to be seen as a woman	Arriving at a comfortable place with cross-dressing	
Having a sense of wholeness as a different kind of man			

FEELING AND OFTEN EXPRESSING A MALE GENDER
IDENTITY FROM A YOUNG AGE

As discussed in chapter 2, many of the study participants who were assigned female at birth and who currently identify as FTM individuals or as men began to feel that they were male, or at least different from females, from their earliest memories; almost all felt male by the time they reached puberty. Most of the transsexual male respondents initially did not see how they were different from other boys and were disbelieving when adults began to treat them as girls. For example, "Rickey," a nineteen-year-old white and American Indian (Cherokee) man, remembers playing with other male children from the time that he was four years old and "didn't understand why everyone would put things in terms of 'me' and 'them.'" But after a few years of being told that he was a girl, Rickey was "painfully aware that [he] wasn't the same as them, and [he] could never really accept that." He states: "I would deny it until I couldn't breathe, but it never made any difference to anyone else."

Like Rickey, Robert knew he was a boy since he was three or four years old and was confused when adults tried to dress him as a girl. "I alternated doubting my sanity or their honesty or whether something weird happened," he recalls. "I was afraid I was insane and would never be able to live a full life. The world was this gigantic fraud and everyone in it, even the most loving people around me in childhood, didn't love me—they loved something they made up."

REPRESSING OR HIDING ONE'S MALE GENDER IDENTITY
IN THE FACE OF HOSTILITY AND/OR ISOLATION

The opposition that Rickey and Robert encountered when they expressed a male gender identity was common among the transsexual male participants. Although about one-third of the respondents indicated that they were allowed or even encouraged to be "tomboys" as children, they often experienced increasing pressure from family and friends to act in traditionally feminine ways as they grew older. Typically, any tolerance for gender nonconformity ended when they reached puberty. Many of the transsexual male participants thus felt forced into a female identity and hid or repressed their sense of themselves as male during adolescence. One of the respondents, Kyle, a white man in his early twenties, remembers feeling alone when all of his tomboy friends were becoming more feminine in middle school. "I wanted to stay a tomboy," he states. "I didn't want to become girly, I wanted to become more manly. But I got teased relentlessly so I tried to be girly. I forced it on myself and got more and more bitter by it."

Other interviewees likewise felt angry and depressed about trying to be someone they were not. "John," a white thirty-nine-year-old, sought to be feminine as a teenager but knew "it was a mask." He says: "I looked like a beautiful female but felt more and more terrible as I got complements as such. In eighth grade, I discovered alcohol, which I then tried to cure my pain with all throughout high school and college."

THINKING OF ONESELF AS LESBIAN BUT REALIZING OVER TIME IT WAS NOT A GOOD FIT

Exhibiting some typically masculine traits and beginning to date women, "John" thought that he was a butch lesbian in college. However, he "soon realized that [he] was nothing like them" because they saw themselves as women and he considered himself male. "I was not butch at all, just a regular guy."

Many of the transsexual male participants who are attracted to women had a similar experience. More than three-fourths of the twenty-seven transsexual men interviewed face-to-face or by telephone indicated that they had identified as lesbian or as a "dyke" before acknowledging themselves as transgender. Other researchers (Devor 1997b; Girshick 2008; Rubin 2003) have likewise found that most of the transsexual men they surveyed initially thought of themselves as lesbians, particularly as butch lesbians, and/or were part of lesbian communities. More than 80 percent of the FTM participants in Devor's (1997b) study assumed lesbian roles, although about one-third did not use the word "lesbian" to describe themselves. All but one of the FTM individuals initially interviewed by Rubin (2003) had lesbian pasts, leading him to seek out additional participants who did not have histories of relationships with women.

Some of the transsexual men whom we surveyed initially felt that a lesbian identity was the best way to characterize their lives. Not only did it explain their interest in women, but it also gave them the freedom to present in more traditionally masculine ways, such as by having short hair and wearing "male" clothing. "In my late teens, I identified as lesbian because I decided that that was a way it was okay for me to like girls," Michael S. remembers. "In my late thirties, I finally accepted that I am transsexual and began presenting and living as male, later going through name change and hormones."

Nathan, a forty-nine-year-old African American man, had likewise come out as lesbian when he recognized that he was attracted to women. But the women whom he dated identified as heterosexual at the time and saw him as male. The relationships did not work out when the women began to identify as lesbians and expected to be involved with someone like themselves. Despite referring to himself as lesbian, Nathan could not relate to them as female or "pass as a woman emotionally."

For Masen, identifying as lesbian and being able to express his gender as he wanted was "an important step in [his] gender journey." Although he eventually realized that there was more to his gender than being a butch woman, he felt that a lesbian identity was "closer to the path [he] needed to be on." It was "an important benchmark or milestone that helped [him] get where [he] needed to go."

Some participants who were attracted to women did not identify as lesbians because both they and their partners saw them as men. It did not matter that they had female bodies. Others did not have female partners, despite being attracted exclusively to women, because they knew that they were not lesbians and did not want to be considered as such by partners just because of their female anatomies. Mark, for example, became a loner beginning in his teen years because he did not want to be in relationships in which he would be treated as female. Unhappy in a society that could not recognize him as he saw himself, Mark turned to alcohol and other drugs as a coping mechanism until he learned more about transsexuality in his late thirties and realized that he could transition.

REALIZING THAT THERE ARE FTM INDIVIDUALS
AND THAT TRANSITIONING IS POSSIBLE

Most of the transsexual male participants who first came out as lesbians did so because it was the identity most readily available to them at the time. Growing up before the Internet made information more accessible and before much had appeared in print about FTM individuals, these respondents did not know about transgender people or had heard only of MTF individuals. Among the transsexual participants interviewed face-to-face or by telephone, nearly half of the FTM people (as compared with about a quarter of the MTF people) reported initially lacking information about others like themselves—including knowledge that transitioning was possible. Among the transsexual men who participated in Devor's (1997b) study, about three-fourths had some knowledge of male-to-female transsexuality during their childhood or teen years, but few learned about female-to-male transsexuality until later in their lives.

When they found out about FTM individuals, many of the transsexual men we interviewed changed how they identified and began to consider transitioning. Some, like Pat, lived most of their lives as butch lesbians before realizing that FTM individuals existed and that they could see themselves as men. "That I could be an FTM wasn't in my perspective. It never hit my mind," Pat states. He started to identify as lesbian in high school in the late 1940s but never felt comfortable around lesbians. Looking back now, he acknowledges that he was not comfortable with himself. After transitioning in his sixties, Pat felt a "huge weight went off." Finally, he "could relax and be [him]self."

Some of the transsexual male participants who were attracted to other men likewise struggled to understand themselves. Tristan, a white forty-three-year-old, began to self-identify as a gay man in his early twenties, but "lived publicly in the role of a heterosexual woman for many years because [he] didn't realize that transition was possible." Not until he learned about FTM individuals through the Internet in his late thirties did he begin to tell other people that he was male and present in more traditionally masculine ways.

Because of the Internet and the growing body of material published by and about FTM individuals since the 1990s, transsexual men today can more readily obtain information and are less likely to spend years being unaware of the existence of others like themselves. Kyle, for example, first learned about FTM individuals when he was seventeen years old. His girlfriend at the time wondered why Kyle was living as a woman if he felt that he was male and sent him links to FTM websites. Until then, he says, "it never occurred to me that I could actually live as a guy."

LEARNING ABOUT AND MEETING OTHER TRANSSEXUAL MEN

Many of the transsexual male participants realized that they could be FTM individuals through meeting another FTM person. Others initially learned about transsexual men through various media and then sought to get to know other FTM individuals, often by connecting with someone they encountered online, through a friend or family member, or in a support group. Two-thirds of the FTM interviewees discussed the importance of other transsexual men in their identity process, and nearly 60 percent indicated that the Internet, books, and/or the news media played a critical role. These findings are in line with the results of other studies. Examining the role of the mass media in the identification processes of transsexual men, Peter Ringo (2002) finds that books, the Internet, and television most affected participants' decisions to come out to themselves or others. In another study, Katherine Rachlin (1999) finds that the most important influences on transsexual men in deciding whether to have genital reconstructive surgery were contact with other FTMs and publications by members of the FTM community.

Nathan, a transsexual man whom we interviewed, first met another transsexual man via a friend; the person became a role model, providing Nathan with information and support as he transitioned. Another participant, "Paul," also considers knowing another FTM person to have been pivotal in his decision to live full-time as a man. His parents had some FTM friends, so he first learned about transsexual men at a young age and did not face a difficult struggle when he chose to transition in his twenties. "It was mostly as easy as pie for me," he remembers.

OVERCOMING DENIAL AND INTERNALIZED GENDERISM
TO ACCEPT ONESELF AS MALE

However, some of the transsexual male respondents did struggle to accept themselves. One such individual was Rej, an Asian American man in his early twenties, who identified as genderqueer before coming out as a transsexual man. He states: "The reason why I identified as a genderqueer initially was because of my own internalized transphobia. It was extremely difficult to shed and purge out all of the negative feelings/ideas attached to being transgender. I, in a way, looked down upon transgender people in the very beginning. So to admit to myself I was one was a long and difficult stage." Rej was able to overcome his anti-transsexual attitudes in part by attending a transsexual male support group and meeting other transsexual men.

TAKING HORMONES AND HAVING TOP SURGERY
TO LOOK MORE LIKE SELF-IMAGE

The vast majority of the transsexual male participants viewed taking testosterone and having chest reconstruction surgery as critical to their identity development, because doing so enabled them to be seen more readily by others as men. After a short time of being on hormones, they developed thicker facial and body hair, deeper voices, and greater muscle mass; as a result, they often began to look little different from other men. The extent to which changing their bodies was important to some of the transsexual male respondents was demonstrated by their ability to remember the exact date they began hormones and/or had top surgery. The FTM individuals typically traced the start of their transitions to when they began altering their bodies.

Of the sixty-three transsexual men interviewed by phone, by e-mail, or in person who provided information about their process of transitioning, fifty-six (87 percent) were on or about to start taking testosterone. Two others planned to begin hormones sometime in the near future, when they had amassed enough money and/or had the requisite therapy. The amount of time that participants had been taking testosterone ranged from a few months to seventeen years, with a mean of slightly more than four years. In Devor's (1997b) study, 84 percent of the transsexual men—all of whom were living as men at the time of his research—were receiving hormone therapy, on average for six-and-a-half years.

Five of the FTM individuals we interviewed were neither on hormones nor about to begin taking them soon. One of these participants, Anthony, had previously taken testosterone but stopped because he no longer had the means to pay for it. He has since decided not to resume hormone therapy, believing that he "doesn't need to be an über guy to be who I am." More important to Anthony was having top surgery so that he could feel comfortable in his body.

Chest reconstruction was also a high priority for many of the other transsexual male interviewees. Thirty-nine (62 percent) had either had or were scheduled for top surgery, and twelve (19 percent) were planning to have the procedure once they had saved enough money. Three (5 percent) indicated that they did not need to change their appearance because they have small breasts and so were able to achieve a more male-contoured chest through weightlifting. The remaining nine respondents are currently not pursuing top surgery for medical or personal reasons or because they have just begun to transition and are still considering it as an option. Other research involving FTM individuals has likewise reported high rates of top surgery. For example, 76 percent of the participants in Devor's (1997b) study and more than half of the participants in Girshick's (2008) study had undergone the procedure.

In contrast, genital or bottom surgery was not important to most of the transsexual male respondents. Frequently given reasons for this attitude include the high cost, what respondents perceived as inadequate results of some of the procedures, and a feeling that they did not need a penis to be men. Only four (6 percent) of the sixty-three interviewees had had a metoidioplasty ("freeing up" of the clitoris to function as a penis), and only one (1.5 percent) had had a phalloplasty (construction of a penis). Few others expressed a desire for bottom surgery in the foreseeable future, given their life and financial circumstances and the current state of the procedure.

Devor's (1997b) findings were similar: two (4 percent) of the participants in his study had had a metoidioplasty and four (9 percent) had had a phalloplasty. Even Rachlin (1999), who studied FTM individuals who had considered genital reconstructive surgery, found that few had gone forward with either procedure (respectively 2 and 11 percent) at the time of her research. Most had rejected bottom surgery because of the inauthenticity and unattractiveness of the results, the risks and complications, and the lack of phallic functionality. Given that many transsexual men do not have genital surgery, Rachlin concludes that "restricting the definition of an FTM to someone who requests a risky, costly, [and] often technologically inadequate surgery is unrealistic."

WHETHER AND WHEN TO TELL OTHERS, AND DEVELOPING
NEW RELATIONSHIPS AFTER DISCLOSURE

The disclosure that someone is transgender and is planning or starting to transition often placed a strain, at least initially, on relationships with family members, coworkers, friends, and partners—especially if the other people were surprised by the revelation. The extent to which respondents' relationships were affected varied, but few close relationships escaped unchanged. In a sense, the participants had to establish new relationships with the people they knew because others did not know their "true selves."

After transitioning, most of the transsexual men surveyed were readily seen by others as men and could choose whether or not to tell new friends and acquaintances about their female-assigned pasts. Some of the respondents were open about their transsexual histories, considering it a part of their identity and often wanting to educate cisgender people about transgender issues. Others sought to leave their previous lives behind them. Now that they could finally be themselves and be recognized as men, they did not want to provide an opportunity for people to think of them as less than other men. As "Aaron," a white and Latino man, states, "once someone knows that I am FTM then they find it hard to treat me as simply male without thinking about my female past or wondering about my genitals." For this reason, he generally does not disclose to people he meets, but this approach has presented difficulties for him, too, because he has many friends from before he transitioned. "It is a delicate balance to deal with those who know about my trans status and those who don't."

Another difficulty faced by many of the transsexual male participants was how and when to tell potential partners about being transgender. "Dating post-transition has been very problematic for me," states Michael W., a forty-two-year-old man. He goes on: "I'm pretty outgoing in general, but when it comes to dating, I am very shy, and really struggle with the whole disclosure issue. More often than not, I pass up potential dates with straight women just so I don't have to deal with it. It feels like lower surgery might alleviate some of that frustration, but I won't really know for sure until it happens . . . if it happens."

HAVING A SENSE OF WHOLENESS AS A DIFFERENT KIND OF MAN

Since few of the transsexual male participants saw bottom surgery as a viable option for at least the near future, respondents developed a sense of themselves as a different kind of man—a man who had been born and raised female and who still had elements of a "female" body. They did not feel that these distinctions made them "incomplete" or less "real" than other men. "My masculinity was so tested by being born female," states Burton, a thirty-three-year-old white man. "It cannot be taken away from me." Like many of the transsexual male participants, Burton defines his gender as how he feels about himself, rather than how he grew up or how he might physically compare to other men.

Echoing these sentiments, Gavriel, a twenty-eight-year-old Iranian American, describes his transsexual past as "another way of being a man." He identifies "first and foremost as a man" but, recognizing that his transsexual history is relevant and meaningful, he refers to himself as "a man with trans experiences." Since transitioning, Gavriel has felt a sense of wholeness; he can embrace both his masculinity and his femininity. Previously, he could not embrace his femininity without being seen as female.

Other transsexual male participants also felt complete once they had transitioned or were in the process of doing so. Masen, for example, described feeling "wholly in [his] body" more than ever before, and Will expressed relief that he was beginning to address "this hole all [his] life" in himself. Will characterizes his life today as "the best [he's] ever felt emotionally and mentally."

MALE-TO-FEMALE TRANSSEXUAL MILESTONES

The study participants who were assigned male at birth and who currently identify as MTF individuals, or as women, often experienced many of the same milestones as the transsexual male respondents but from a female standpoint. They typically felt and often expressed a female gender identity from a young age, repressed or hid their female gender identity in the face of hostility and/or isolation, benefited from getting to know about and meet other transsexual women, overcame denial and internalized genderism to accept themselves as female, took hormones and sometimes had surgery to look more like their self-image, decided whether and when to tell others and developed new relationships after disclosure, and achieved a sense of wholeness as "real" women. However, the two groups did vary with respect to some milestones and often experienced the same milestones differently.

FEELING AND OFTEN EXPRESSING A FEMALE
GENDER IDENTITY FROM A YOUNG AGE

About equal percentages of the transsexual men (67 percent) and transsexual women (62 percent) who were interviewed by telephone or face-to-face felt from a young age that they were different from the gender assigned to them at birth. Most of the FTM individuals (82 percent) stated that they were able to act on their feelings by taking on traditionally male roles in play and in relationships with other children. In contrast, only a minority (37 percent) of the MTF individuals said that they could assume traditionally female gender roles, because such behavior was often discouraged or disallowed by their families. Presumably, the parents thought that their male-assigned children would become gay and immediately sought to prevent it, whereas the female-assigned children were often allowed to be tomboys without concerns being raised initially about their sexuality. Roughly equal percentages of transsexual women (82 percent) and transsexual men (78 percent) indicated that they dressed and presented as the gender they felt themselves to be, but all of the MTF individuals had to do so secretly.

None of the twenty-eight transsexual women who discussed the reactions of their families in our telephone or face-to-face interviews received any acceptance for presenting or acting female growing up. On the contrary, three (11 percent) reported that they were physically or sexually assaulted for doing so, and five (18 percent) others were sent to therapists or were institutionalized to be "cured." For example, Diana T., a white forty-nine-year-old, had little chance to be herself as a child. Soon after she began cross-dressing at age six or seven, she was caught by her mother and subsequently whipped by her father. She was more careful about cross-dressing thereafter but was still caught a number of times and severely punished. Eventually, her parents grew tired of beating her and locked her in a room instead, what she calls being "treated like an animal." These experiences made it difficult for Diana to accept herself, and by her twenties she was using drugs "to go numb" and subconsciously, she now believes, to try to kill herself.

When she was ten years old, Mary was caught cross-dressing by her mother, who sent her to a psychiatrist despite Mary's insistence that she did not want to be a girl. The experience "scared [her] to death" and led Mary to hide her "true self" even more. A couple years later, her stepmother discovered her cross-dressing and sent Mary to another psychiatrist, who threatened to turn her in to the police for stealing her mother's and sister's clothes if she did not stop cross-dressing. Mary learned to lie to this therapist, too. She "got good at lying" and denied to herself and to others that she was female for the next thirty years. Like Diana, she used drugs and alcohol to avoid facing her unhappiness at pretending to be a man.

By comparison, nearly half (47 percent) of the seventeen transsexual men who addressed the gender socialization of their families stated that their parents were lenient, allowing them to be tomboys well into adolescence. Three other respondents (18 percent) specifically indicated that their parents encouraged them to be more stereotypically female but did not push them very hard. Even families that more firmly sought to have their transsexual male children act and dress in more traditionally feminine ways did not punish them harshly to try to force them to change.

REPRESSING OR HIDING ONE'S FEMALE GENDER IDENTITY IN THE FACE OF HOSTILITY AND/OR ISOLATION

Given the greater hostility and sense of isolation felt by many of the transsexual female participants growing up, it is not surprising that they were more likely than the transsexual male participants to have felt guilty about or to have denied or repressed their gender feelings. Thirteen (22 percent) of the transsexual female telephone and face-to-face interviewees stated that they had been ashamed of this part of themselves, or had thought it was sinful and prayed to be able to stop cross-dressing. In contrast, only one transsexual male interviewee said that he had felt guilty about being male-identified. Nearly twice as many of the MTF as FTM respondents (42 versus 22 percent) indicated that they sought to hide or overcome their gender feelings by trying to fit into traditional gender roles.

The transsexual female interviewees sought to deny their gender identities in a number of ways that were rarely mentioned by the transsexual male interviewees. For example, ten (17 percent) of the transsexual women described feeling that they would be "cured" of their sense of themselves as female by falling in love or marrying; none of the transsexual men expressed this sentiment. The transsexual women were also more likely to indicate that they tried to escape from their "gender troubles" through abusing alcohol or other drugs (mentioned by six MTF individuals but just one FTM individual) or by burying themselves in hobbies or work (mentioned by five MTF individuals but by none of the FTM individuals). One of the transsexual women who used the latter survival mechanism was Lisa, a white fifty-two-year-old who channeled what she calls her "internal crisis" into music and became a rock guitarist. In a 2006 interview, she stated: "My guitar has saved me from death. . . . Back [in] 1965 when I decided to play, then through the '70s, '80s, and beyond, I was absolutely clueless about my gender issues . . . nowhere to turn, no one to relate to. My instrument was all there was. I had to relate to it. I hid myself in it."[2]

Other transsexual women sought to escape from their feminine feelings through what George Brown (1988) describes as a "flight into hypermasculinity." Brown, a military psychiatrist who studied MTF individuals with extensive service backgrounds, found that they commonly joined the military in an attempt to "become real men" and that some even volunteered for high-risk combat assignments in seeking to prove their "manliness" to themselves and others (529). Other research (Gagné et al. 1997; Samons 2009) has also recognized this phenomenon.

A number of the MTF people whom we interviewed likewise joined the military as a way to avoid facing their gender feelings and in the hope that the experience would, as Shirley desired, "make more of a man out of [her]." Shirley, a white sixty-one-year-old, entered the Air Force to "purge" her feminine self. Her sense of being female persisted, however, which led her to leave the military and take a job in which she could travel and be a woman while away from home. A few of the MTF interviewees were drafted for the Korean or Vietnam Wars. Some of these respondents saw it as an opportunity to try to overcome their feminine feelings, while others coped with not being able to act on their feelings until they were discharged.

LEARNING ABOUT AND MEETING OTHER TRANSSEXUAL WOMEN

Until the last ten to fifteen years, most of the information available about transsexuality was about transsexual women. For this reason, the MTF participants were more likely than the FTM participants (48 versus 28 percent) to report knowing about others like themselves when they began to question their gender identity. Many of the older transsexual female respondents learned about what they were experiencing by reading the autobiographies of Christine Jorgensen, Jan Morris, and/or Renée Richards. For Liz, a fifty-two-year-old white woman, a key moment was discovering Jorgensen's autobiography in the library when she was twelve or thirteen years old. She recalls thinking, "Wow, that's my story." From her earliest memories, Liz had wanted to be a girl. Now she finally had a name for how she felt and "knew [she] wasn't the only person in the world who felt this way."

Perhaps because of the relatively greater resources historically available to MTF individuals, our transsexual female interviewees often attached less importance to meeting others like themselves in their process of self-acceptance than did the transsexual male interviewees. Fewer than a third of the MTF respondents mentioned knowing others like themselves as a part of their identity development, as compared with two-thirds of the transsexual male respondents. Still, for some transsexual women, meeting other MTF individuals played a critical role in their transitioning. Jennifer Z., for example, cites her involvement with a transsexual female support group as enabling her to recognize that she was not alone as a male-assigned woman and that "transitioning [was] not beyond her reach, and thus, neither [was] true happiness with being able to finally be [her]self." Another interviewee, Nikki, also benefited from joining a local support group, where she met an MTF individual who became her "big sister" and a role model. Through knowing her, Nikki accepted that she was a transsexual woman and "began to forgive [her]self for the years of hatred and denial."

RECOGNIZING ONESELF AS TRANSSEXUAL RATHER THAN AS A CROSS-DRESSER

Meeting other MTF individuals was especially important for the transsexual women who were in denial or who were unsure about being transsexual. The vast majority of the transsexual female phone and face-to-face interviewees expressed their gender feelings by cross-dressing from a young age, and some believed that they were cross-dressers. Twenty-three interviewees (38 percent) mentioned that they first identified as cross-dressers before realizing or admitting to themselves that their female gender feelings went beyond expressing a feminine side. They began to identify as transsexual when they recognized that they never wanted to stop being women. For Shirley, a sign that she was more than a cross-dresser was taking the opportunity afforded by Halloween to wear a dress publicly and acknowledging to herself that she "didn't want to take it off."

Many of the transsexual female respondents who were interviewed by e-mail also initially thought of themselves as cross-dressers. Jacqueline attributes her first believing that she was a cross-dresser, and not an MTF, to societal and family stigmas and a fear of surgery. But as her knowledge about transsexuality grew, "just cross-dressing [became] never enough; [she] always wanted 'more.'" Julie Marie, a white fifty-four-year-old, reached a similar point in her life. Even though she had felt herself to be female from as early as she could remember, Julie Marie denied her feelings and insisted that she was a cross-dresser because "that's all [she] wanted to be." Married and with three children, she feared losing her family if she "followed [her] heart." However, she came to conclude that she could never be content simply cross-dressing. "It's either transition or I'll die inside," Julie Marie realized. "Once I decided to transition I felt a huge weight off my shoulders and began to feel at peace inside for the first time in my life."

OVERCOMING DENIAL AND INTERNALIZED GENDERISM TO ACCEPT ONESELF AS FEMALE

Like Julie Marie, a number of the transsexual female participants told moving stories about accepting themselves as female. The following is the account of fifty-six-year-old Sheila.

I have always known that I was female but didn't know any better, as my peers and adults around me told me I was male. I believed them and tried hard to be who I was supposed to be. It didn't work, as I had a mental breakdown. When I accepted myself for whom I have always known, I became a happier person and calmer. I don't wake up every morning wondering if today is the day I kill myself and wondering why I am in this body.

The extent to which some of the transsexual female interviewees were in denial is demonstrated by the drastic circumstances under which they came to accept themselves. Five MTF individuals stated that a major traumatic experience (for three, a near-death experience) led them finally to act on their gender feelings. For example, being nearly killed twice in the Gulf War made Sarafina, a white and Latina thirty-eight-year-old, realize that "life was too short" to continue to deny being transsexual. In contrast, none of the FTM interviewees indicated that a crisis had played a critical role in their decision to transition.

TAKING HORMONES AND PERHAPS HAVING SURGERY
TO LOOK MORE LIKE SELF-IMAGE

As with the transsexual male participants, the vast majority of the transsexual female respondents considered beginning to take hormones as an important milestone that marked a turning point in their lives as women. Of the sixty MTF individuals interviewed by telephone or in person, fifty-two (87 percent) were on or about to start hormones—the same percentage as among the FTM interviewees. The average amount of time that the MTF individuals had been on hormones was about six years, as compared with about four years for the FTM individuals.

However, the two groups differed significantly with regard to having bottom surgery. Sixteen (27 percent) of the transsexual female telephone and in-person interviewees had already had or were scheduled to have a vaginoplasty (construction of a vagina), and another five (8 percent) were planning to have the procedure within the next year. A few of the respondents chose not to have gender confirmation surgery (GCS) because they felt it was unnecessary to becoming a woman, because of age or poor health, or because they were concerned about sexual functioning afterward. But most of the transsexual women who had not already had GCS wanted to do so; however, they could not afford it at the present time or were prevented by other life circumstances from transitioning. A greater percentage of the MTF than FTM individuals interviewed (28 versus 15 percent) reported that they encountered delays or were unable to transition because of their particular situations, including the negative effects (or feared negative effects) on their children, romantic partners, and/or birth families; hostility from local medical professionals; and concerns about the reactions of people where they live or work. Whereas only a few of the FTM interviewees were parents at the time that they began to consider transitioning, about half of the MTF interviewees had children. Twenty percent of the FTM parents indicated that they postponed taking hormones and having GCS until their children were adults and on their own—so as not to interfere with their lives or lose custody or visitation rights in divorce proceedings. Other MTF participants waited until their spouses or birth families adjusted to the idea or until they could separate from them.

Even when the people closest to them were encouraging, some of the transsexual female respondents still faced personal challenges to transitioning. One of these individuals is Rachel G., a forty-seven-year-old woman who, despite having the strong support of her wife and father, does not present as female full-time at this point because she does not always feel safe doing so in the conservative area where she lives. Still, she has sought to educate the people around her, including local doctors and therapists, about transgender issues and estimates that she now expresses herself as female "95 percent of the time."

The transsexual female participants often faced several impediments at once. For instance, before Shelby can begin to transition she must resolve her marriage, work out her relationships with her three children, and find a new job (she works for a law firm that would be hostile to her as a woman). Facing similar obstacles, Michelle P. concluded that the personal costs of transitioning are too great. She states: "I did go as far as researching hormones years back and buying them online. . . . I had to decide to stop because if I developed much more, there was no way I could live in both worlds. I'd have to come out to everyone, lose my job/home, and I couldn't make that jump to go female 24/7 as much as I want to." Kim L., who identifies "somewhere between a CD [cross-dresser] and a TS [transsexual]," made the same decision. "If I do more than CD, I will lose my love and family," she says. "At this time, that is too high a price."

WHETHER AND WHEN TO TELL OTHERS, AND DEVELOPING
NEW RELATIONSHIPS AFTER DISCLOSURE

Like the transsexual male participants, the transsexual female respondents who chose to transition encountered a wide range of reactions to the disclosure. Of the forty-nine transsexual women who discussed their relationship history during our telephone or in-person interviews, forty-four were married to a woman at the time they recognized themselves as an MTF and/or began to transition. More than two-thirds of these marriages subsequently ended, often because their partners did not feel comfortable being involved with another woman. In a few instances, the transsexual women themselves sought a divorce, recognizing that they needed to focus on transitioning or that they had married largely to try to overcome their sense of themselves as female. Other transsexual women remained in denial or continued to believe that marriage to the "right woman" would "cure" them, even after their first marriages had ended as a result of their cross-gender identity. Six of the MTF participants had been divorced twice, and two had been divorced three times, because of concerns related to their transsexuality.

Some of the wives at first voiced support for their spouses' transitions but realized over time that they could not accept them as women or were uncomfortable being seen by others as having a female partner. After her first marriage ended, Kayle, a white fifty-year-old interviewee, married a woman whom she indicates was "initially very supportive" of her gender identity, which included buying her "women's" clothing. Unlike many of the other survey participants' wives, Kayle's partner had been involved with other women previously, so Kayle thought that her transition would not be an issue. But after they had a child, Kayle's wife insisted that she stop presenting as female, which Kayle did. However, Kayle's wife still ended the relationship and left her for a cisgender woman. Until recently, one heard few stories about MTFs whose relationships survived their transitions. Indeed, the medical establishment for decades dictated that transsexual women who were married and seeking to transition obtain a divorce from their wives before they would be eligible for surgery (Denny 2006). In the last few years, though, narratives of MTFs who have stayed married or partnered have become more common in the lore of the transgender community and the subject of two texts: one by transsexual women and men (O'Keefe & Fox 2008) and another by the wives of transsexual women and female-presenting CDs (Erhardt 2007).

Thirteen of the MTFs we interviewed reported that they and their wives have remained together through their transitions. In most of these instances, the disclosure of the participants' crossgender feelings at least initially placed a great strain on their marriages. The relationships ultimately survived, but not all fully recovered. Three of the MTF respondents indicated that their marriages have become platonic because their wives do not want to be sexual with another woman. "Carol," for example, stated that she and her wife are no longer intimate but continue to be "good friends." She wishes that she had intimacy in her life but is not willing to forgo her marriage of thirty-three years.

A few of the interviewees indicated that their marriages actually improved after they came out as MTF individuals, since they became easier to get along with when they could be themselves and no longer had to hide or repress their gender identities. Like a majority of the married transsexual female respondents, Mary initially kept her gender feelings from her wife and children and, in retrospect, realizes that she "took out [her] frustration on [her] family without knowing it." Finally, when "the pain was getting to be too much," Mary told her wife and was relieved to find that she was completely supportive. Her wife realized that Mary had no choice in being transgender and "accepted her for her."

Allason, in contrast, told her wife before their marriage. They were friends for several years first and have been married for nine years. Allason's spouse is a female-bodied cross-dresser, which enables her to understand Allason's experiences. According to Allason, she "loves [her] for who [she] is."

A difficulty that the transsexual female participants encountered more often than did the transsexual men was being perceived as transgender in new relationships. Some of the MTF individuals who sought to present as female were still recognized, at times, as having been assigned male at birth because they were taller and had larger hands, more extensive facial hair, and deeper voices than most women and exhibited masculine facial features and prominent Adam's apples. As a result, they had no choice about whether or when to disclose their transsexual histories. This situation was especially common for the transsexual women who had made fewer visible changes to their bodies, such as taking hormones, having electrolysis, and undergoing a chondrolaryngoplasty (tracheal shave) and facial feminization surgery.

Many of the MTF individuals in this position had problems finding romantic partners; they may also have faced difficulties obtaining employment or being promoted or postponed transitioning at their workplaces for fear of discrimination. Rhiannon, a forty-eight-year-old woman of American Indian (Cree, Anashinabe, Assinboine, and Metis) and Celtic ancestry, experienced hardships in both areas. Since beginning hormones twenty years ago, she has not been able to find other women who are romantically interested in her. Moreover, she has not been able to save money for procedures that would make her look more traditionally female and might make her appealing to more women. She has an entry-level customer service job and has been passed over for advancement for several years, she believes, because of anti-transgender prejudice.

HAVING A SENSE OF WHOLENESS EVEN WHEN UNABLE TO BE SEEN AS A WOMAN

Although the respondents were not specifically asked how they currently feel about themselves, many of the transsexual female interviewees stated that they are much happier today after transitioning because they are comfortable in their bodies and are finally able to be seen by others as they have long felt inside. Even the participants who were sometimes or frequently "read" as transgender (because they retain traditionally male body characteristics) still often felt a sense of inner peace and expressed relief that they could now be themselves.

Like the FTM interviewees who recognized that not having a penis did not make them any less of a man, many MTF interviewees stated that they did not feel less "real" or less "whole" for not always appearing like other women.

"At six-feet-four and a size twenty-two, I hardly expect to pass as a genetic woman," states Barbara, an MTF individual who continues to present as male at work. But her inability to look like most other women does not deter her from being comfortable and self-assured in public as female, which includes attending an Episcopal church with her wife and speaking to high school and college classes. "By being open and honest and somewhat self-deprecating, I have made many friends. I have also been blessed to be invited into what I can only call sacred women's space and a community of faith and friendship."

FEMALE-PRESENTING CROSS-DRESSER MILESTONES

The MTF and cross-dressing participants often had similar early life trajectories. As already stated, many of the MTF interviewees indicated that they first saw themselves as cross-dressers before recognizing that they identified as female, rather than just feeling a need to present as female. The lives of the cross-dressing respondents diverged from the lives of the transsexual female respondents in the extent to which they expressed themselves as women; the cross-dressers typically did not permanently change their bodies to appear more traditionally feminine. However, like many of the MTF participants, the cross-dressing participants often repressed or hid their gender identity in the face of opposition. But frequently by meeting others like themselves, they overcame their internalized genderism and stopped denying their "true selves."

As with many of the transsexual female participants, almost all of the CD survey respondents who had been assigned male at birth began to cross-dress as children. Among the nineteen CD individuals interviewed by telephone or in person, the mean age at which they reported having their first cross-dressing experience was seven; this is one-and-a-half years younger than indicated by participants in an earlier study of female-presenting cross-dressers (Bullough & Bullough 1997). A few of the respondents were first cross-dressed by female family members or initially had permission to dress in their clothing; the rest discovered cross-dressing on their own, typically with the clothing of female relatives. But no matter how they started cross-dressing, the CD interviewees, like the MTF interviewees, learned over time that they needed to hide it from others or face punishment.

However, only a few of our nineteen CD interviewees were discovered as cross-dressers—often because they kept, and their families found, a stash of "female" clothing. Most were extremely cautious so as to avoid being detected. "Every time my parents went out to the store, I would drop whatever I was doing and head for the lingerie drawer in my parents' bedroom," remembers Susan, a sixty-six-year-old cross-dresser. "I would carefully calculate just how much time I had to explore. Somehow I was never caught." If Susan's mother did notice that her clothing had been worn or moved, she did not say anything. In her teens, Susan was able to collect a few items of her own through "the lame old story about buying 'for [her] sister,'" which enabled her to avoid the risks associated with wearing her mother's clothes and to cross-dress more frequently.

BUYING OR OBTAINING ONE'S OWN "WOMEN'S" CLOTHING

A point of divergence between individuals who were cross-dressers and the transsexual women who expressed their sense of themselves as female through cross-dressing was that many of the CD individuals viewed obtaining their own "women's" clothes and expanding their cross-dressing to be a significant milestone. It was mentioned by 79 percent (fifteen) of the cross-dressers but by none of the sixty MTF individuals interviewed by telephone or face-to-face. The importance that the cross-dressers attached to acquiring their own wardrobe was reflected in their frequent ability to remember the time and circumstances under which they did so. Wondering how she was going to obtain "women's" clothing of her own, Michelle G., a thirty-three-year-old white cross-dresser, recalls being with a group of friends in high school who were the last ones to leave a waterslide and finding a pair of women's panties on the floor in the locker area. "I grabbed them, loved them, and then bought my own," she states. Over the years, she has gradually shopped for other "women's" clothes, sometimes bringing them home to wear secretly but more often simply trying on items in stores.

REPRESSING THE DESIRE TO CROSS-DRESS
AND PURGING CLOTHING BECAUSE OF SHAME

Like many of the MTF interviewees, many of the CD respondents interviewed by telephone or in person felt ashamed about cross-dressing because of the severe social stigma against male-assigned individuals wearing traditionally women's clothing. Almost half (47 percent) of the CD participants indicated that they felt guilty about their behavior and had disposed of all of their "female" garments at least once. Two earlier studies of cross-dressers (Prince & Bentler 1972; Docter & Prince 1997) find that 69 and 75 percent of the respondents, respectively, had purged. The lower percentage of individuals in our survey who reported having disposed of their "female" clothes may indicate that fewer cross-dressers today experience a prolonged period of shame before accepting this aspect of themselves.

Most of the interviewees who purged subsequently bought new clothing, only to purge again. For some, this cycle of purging and replacing continued for decades. "The hiding, the shame, the guilt, the purging, the resisting, the relapse into buying more clothing and dressing once again, which led to repeating the cycle, plagued my life for the next thirty years," states Michelle S., a cross-dresser in her fifties. "All those thirty years I felt that I was all alone in this obsession and that I was the only heterosexual male in the world who could not resist wearing feminine clothing."

Other CD interviewees likewise felt that they were the only one like themselves—what Cheryl, a sixty-year-old white cross-dresser, describes as being a "total freak of nature." Many despised themselves not only for cross-dressing but also for not being able to stop. "I hated who I was and what I did," Donna states. "I hated that no one knew that I was so screwed up. . . . I resolved myself to the fact that my life, however long I [chose] to continue it, would be such that I was to be forever alone with my pathetic secret."

LEARNING ABOUT AND MEETING OTHER CROSS-DRESSERS

Donna realized that she was by no means the only man who cross-dressed when she went online in 1997 and discovered several discussion groups for cross-dressers. Through being involved in these forums, she recognized that there were many people like herself and that she was not "screwed up." Many of the other cross-dressing participants related similar experiences. They had not had a name for how they felt or had not known that others felt the same way for years or, in some instances, for decades until the advent of the Internet. Sandra, a fifty-seven-year-old cross-dresser, knew she was different from a young age but did not understand what it meant until eleven years ago, when she bought a computer and went online. She "only had Christine Jorgensen and Renée Richards, but [she] knew [she] was not like them and couldn't identify with them." By meeting other cross-dressing individuals, especially other transgender Christians, via the Internet, Sandra was able to start feeling good about herself and realize that being a cross-dresser was not sinful.

OVERCOMING SHAME TO ACCEPT ONESELF AS A CROSS-DRESSER

Meeting other cross-dressers online and/or through CD support groups like Tri-Ess (the Society for the Second Self) enabled many of the CD respondents to begin to accept themselves. Tina M., a fifty-four-year-old cross-dresser, discovered that there were other people like herself when she went online about a decade ago. The experience was very affirming for Tina and led her to an "epiphany" about cross-dressing: "I like it and there is nothing wrong with it. I'm not an evil person. I'm not going to be ashamed anymore." Another cross-dresser, Julie, realized that she faced a choice: either deny her "true nature" and "exist at the lowest level of life" or be herself and "be content and enjoy life." When seen in these terms, the decision was an easy one for her to make, and Julie soon "came to peace with trans issues."

CROSS-DRESSING IN PUBLIC FOR THE FIRST TIME AND ADOPTING A FEMININE NAME

For all nineteen of the CD participants interviewed by phone or in person, going out in public visibly cross-dressed was seen as an important milestone. Suzi explained its significance this way: "Getting out is the biggest step for most 'T' people because the number of possible disasters are infinite. However, once the panic is overcome, the potential for fun is endless." Many of the cross-dressers were extremely frightened the first time that they did so publicly, believing that they would be harassed, assaulted, or outed if they ran into a friend, neighbor, or coworker who did not know they sometimes wore "women's" clothing. Sandy, for example, was more afraid to walk outside cross-dressed than she had been to serve in military combat. But when she did start going out, Sandy relished the opportunity to be herself and found that she had been overly concerned about the likelihood of negative consequences. She admits that it "was almost a disappointment that [she] didn't get anybody's attention."

Once they overcame their initial fears, many of the other interviewees likewise felt a sense of satisfaction and relief in publicly cross-dressing. Susan saw going out as liberating:

The sensation of being out of doors was very special. The openness and airiness of being attired in a skirt, with the clothing swaying with your movements, was extraordinary. Part of it was the clothing. Most of it was the feeling of freedom of being outside. That would come to be a facet of my feminine life that I would particularly treasure. The thrill of being out of doors *en femme* was the ultimate contrast to all of the years in hiding.

Not all of the CD respondents, though, were able or wanted to cross-dress publicly. Some lived and worked in a small town or rural area and felt that there was no place they could go where they would not be recognized or greatly risk being assaulted. If they were far from a large city or did not have the opportunity to do much traveling, they had to be satisfied with cross-dressing in private. Others—like Lynn T., an interviewee who has partly cross-dressed for more than forty years—were content to cross-dress only at home and, when possible, on out-of-town trips and at cross-dressing events and/or support group meetings. A few of the CD participants indicated that they cross-dressed largely in their homes as part of an agreement with their spouses to avoid potential harm to themselves and their families, but most of the interviewees who cross-dressed privately simply felt more comfortable doing so.

For many of the participants, another aspect of being more open with cross-dressing was adopting a feminine name to refer to themselves when cross-dressed, what some described as their "second selves." All but two of the eighty-five cross-dressing individuals interviewed for the study chose to identify themselves using a traditionally female name. Some respondents kept these names largely private, while others were widely known in person and/or online as their female selves. The awareness that their partners or spouses were using a feminine name often reinforced the seriousness of the cross-dressing. For Sandra's wife, "reality hit" when she saw Sandra's signature on an e-mail to a transgender Christian listserv. According to Sandra, "from that point [her wife] realized that there really was a second spirit involved."

WHETHER AND WHEN TO TELL OTHERS, AND DEVELOPING NEW RELATIONSHIPS AFTER DISCLOSURE

Unlike the transsexual individuals who were in the process of transitioning, the cross-dressing participants did not have to disclose that they were transgender. Many sought to do so, however, because they did not want to hide a central part of their lives from their partners and families. But some kept it to themselves, believing that marriage would cure their cross-dressing or that their spouses would leave them if they disclosed. A few of the CD participants were unsure about how to raise the issue, as they did not understand their cross-dressing themselves.

Of the nineteen cross-dressers interviewed by telephone or in person, eighteen are or seek to be involved in relationships with women, and seventeen are (or have been) married to a woman. The wives of these seventeen respondents all knew that their husbands cross-dressed. The participants were almost evenly divided between individuals who told their wives about their cross-dressing before their wedding (35 percent), individuals who disclosed after they were married (35 percent), and individuals whose cross-dressing was discovered by their wives (29 percent).

Seven of the participants were divorced. In six of these instances, the interviewees believed that their cross-dressing either contributed or directly led to the dissolution of their marriages—even when their wives knew at the outset of the relationship. Angie, a fifty-three-year-old transgender individual, told her wife about her cross-dressing before they married. Her wife accepted it and consented, for example, to Angie cross-dressing when they went on vacations or took shopping trips. But after more than twenty-five years of marriage, Angie's wife said that she could no longer live with a transgender husband. Despite Angie's explanation that she could not "remove that part of [her]self" any more than her wife could stop being Italian, they parted soon thereafter.

Four of the CD individuals who were divorced subsequently remarried, so that fourteen (78 percent) of the cross-dressing interviewees who were attracted to women were married at the time of the survey. Four of these participants (29 percent) characterized their wives as accepting or embracing of their cross-dressing, nine (64 percent) described their wives as tolerant, and one (7 percent) considered her wife to be intolerant. By comparison, Docter and Prince (1997) find that 28 percent of the wives in their study were "completely accepting," 47 percent had a "mixed view," and 19 percent were "completely antagonistic."

Most of the CD interviewees who characterized their wives as "accepting" indicated that their spouses enjoyed spending time with them *en femme,* accompanied them to Tri-Ess or other cross-dressing group events, and therefore knew other heterosexual male cross-dressers and their partners. Through meeting these other couples, the wives recognized that their partners were not abnormal for cross-dressing, had other women in a similar situation to turn to for support if needed, and could see that cross-dressing did not have to be an issue in their marriages. Sandra's wife, for example, was devastated when she discovered that Sandra cross-dressed, fearing that her spouse was gay and would leave her. But she became "more comfortable" after attending a local Tri-Ess meeting, where she met other wives with whom she could relate, and the two developed close friendships with other couples who share similar Christian beliefs. According to Sandra, her wife now sees being involved in the Tri-Ess group "as a ministry [with which] she can help."

In contrast, many of the wives who were described as "tolerant" refused to see their spouses cross-dressed or attend cross-dressing group meetings. They fervently wished that they were not married to a cross-dresser but "put up with it," in the words of one of the CD interviewees, to preserve the marriage. "Jessica," a sixty-four-year-old interviewee, finds herself in this situation. She and her wife separated at first because of Jessica's cross-dressing, but they reunited about a year later when her wife was assured that Jessica was not transsexual. However, their relationship remains strained at times. Her wife endures Jessica's cross-dressing as long as she does not have to be "a part of it in any way."

Susan's wife "Jill" was the one "intolerant" wife among the couples who have stayed married. Not only is she adamantly opposed to seeing Susan cross-dressed, she also refuses to discuss the topic; the two have not spoken about Susan's cross-dressing in more than five years. When Susan came to terms with herself as a cross-dresser in 1994 and told her wife, Jill demanded that she move her "female" clothing out of the house. Susan currently has her wardrobe at the house of a longtime friend who lives an hour away. Because she cross-dresses only while on out-of-town trips, Susan does not find this situation to be overly burdensome. But she does feel guilty that she has to sneak away to cross-dress and is sad that she must keep a meaningful aspect of her life from her wife.

ARRIVING AT A COMFORTABLE PLACE WITH CROSS-DRESSING

Some of the CD participants still struggled over whether to disclose their cross-dressing to their partners, and others who had already disclosed had difficulties in their romantic relationships. However, many of the respondents described being comfortable with themselves and with the place that cross-dressing had assumed in their lives. "I can't begin to tell you just how good it felt, to be able to finally express my hidden feminine side," Tina M. stated. "I finally came to terms with my true self. I will no longer deny myself the truth. . . . I know I'm a man, but I can enjoy being a girl."

Angie expressed a similar sentiment, saying that being a cross-dresser "is who and what I am." She is active in a local Tri-Ess chapter and frequently goes out in public cross-dressed, not worrying if others see her as male bodied. When she encounters a negative reaction from someone, Angie seeks to disarm the person through "a smile, a sense of humor, and a recognizable positive self-image"; she does not let hostility affect her sense of herself.

PASSING OF THE TERM "CROSS-DRESSER"?

Overall, the CD respondents were significantly older than the rest of the people who participated in the survey. Among the eighty-five cross-dressing individuals interviewed by telephone, by e-mail, or in person, the majority were in their fifties or older. The youngest CD interviewee was thirty-two years old. Other studies have likewise involved samples of generally older, female-presenting cross-dressers. For example, the mean ages of the cross-dressers surveyed by Richard Schott (1995) and Bonnie and Vern Bullough (1997) were forty-seven and forty-eight years old, respectively. Three studies conducted by Virginia Prince (Docter & Prince 1997; Prince

1962; Prince & Bentler 1972) demonstrate the "aging" of cross-dressing samples. In the first two studies, for which data was gathered in the 1960s, a majority of the participants were under forty years old, and 20 percent of the individuals surveyed in 1972 were in their twenties. Yet among the respondents to the 1997 survey, a majority were older than forty and just 10 percent were less than thirty. Docter and Prince (1997:599) suggest that this age difference may reflect the older membership of the cross-dressing support groups from which they recruited most of their participants; younger cross-dressers are more likely to socialize in bars and other venues where they can cross-dress in public. It could also be that fewer younger transgender people today are choosing to refer to themselves as cross-dressers.

GENDERQUEER MILESTONES

Whereas our survey respondents who identified as cross-dressers were substantially older on average than the rest of the sample, the participants who identified as genderqueer (GQ) or who otherwise described their gender in nonbinary terms were substantially younger overall than the other transgender people surveyed. Of the fourteen genderqueer individuals interviewed, all were younger than fifty and most were in their twenties or early thirties. Autobiographical stories (see, e.g., Diamond 2004; Nestle, Howell, & Wilchins 2002; O'Keefe & Fox 2003; Scott-Dixon 2006) and anecdotal evidence (Beemyn 2008) also suggest that many younger transgender people today are embracing nonbinary or fluid gender identities.

The growing number of transgender youth who are identifying as genderqueers rather than as cross-dressers partly reflects generational changes in terminology or a cohort effect.[3] Younger individuals today who partially or completely cross-dress often choose to describe themselves using what they see as more modern and more gender-transgressive terms, such as "genderqueer," "gender fluid," "bigendered," "third gendered," "androgynous," and "boi." Yet beyond new ways to name transgender experiences, the use of terms like "genderqueer" reflects a growing understanding among individuals who are now coming out as transgender that gender is not a binary concept.

Male-bodied cross-dressers frequently see themselves as having a second, female self that is separate from their male gender identity. Adhering to a two-gender system, they distinguish between being *en femme* (presenting as a woman) and being "in drab" (presenting in their everyday male mode). In contrast, genderqueer individuals identify and express themselves in ways that challenge conventional static, binary constructions of gender. They describe their gender identity as being a combination of female and male; as neither male nor female but as a different gender altogether; or as somewhere "in between" female and male.

Some of the genderqueer participants partly or entirely transitioned by taking hormones, undergoing gender confirmation surgeries, and/or altering their bodies in other ways, such as through electrolysis or bodybuilding. Others did not change their bodies but still destabilized gender categories in their self-expression, such as by dressing as both "female" and "male" in their everyday lives, combining so-called feminine and masculine aspects of appearance, or presenting androgynously. For example, 'Ron, a twenty-eight-year-old multiracial interviewee, enjoys mixing traditionally female and male characteristics. Ze might bind hir breasts and wear "boy's" jeans with a blouse and eye makeup, or ze might wear "men's" clothing and not bind. 'Ron likes "messing with people's heads," so ze is not offended when people often call hir "sir" and "ma'am" in the same breath.

Although the genderqueer respondents expressed their gender identity in a wide variety of ways, they often experienced similar milestones in the process of recognizing and acknowledging themselves as gender different. Among the genderqueer interviewees, some common life moments included feeling and often expressing a gender identity different from their assigned gender from a young age, realizing that genderqueer is a viable identity, deciding on how to present oneself as genderqueer, encountering resistance to their nontraditional gender behavior and/or appearance, not fitting into transgender or LGBT communities, and finding a home within or outside of those communities.

The vast majority (86 percent) of the 111 individuals surveyed who identified as genderqueer had been assigned female at birth, which was also the case for twelve of the fourteen genderqueer interviewees. This disparity may reflect the overall greater leeway in gender expression experienced by the respondents who were raised as women. Like the other female-assigned participants, the female-assigned genderqueer interviewees were often able to assume more traditionally male modes of presentation and behavior as children, and even though many were pressured by peers and family members to act more feminine during adolescence, they did not have to adhere to a narrow range of gender roles.

Many of the female-assigned genderqueer interviewees did not grow up identifying as traditionally female; however, in contrast to the vast majority of FTM interviewees, they also did not think of themselves as male. Esther, for example, knew as a teenager that "[ze] wasn't happy as a 'typical female'" but thought at the time that ze was "just tomboyish." Hir "feelings of not being female" grew even stronger in hir twenties. Yet so, too, did a sense that ze did not want to be male. It was not until Esther learned about the concept of being genderqueer in hir thirties that ze had a better understanding of hir feelings.

Similarly, the male-assigned genderqueer participants who spoke about their childhoods felt and/or acted in traditionally feminine ways growing up but did not identify as female. Daniel, a twenty-eight-year-old respondent, thought of himself as a "Jewish sissy-boy" growing up. Not knowing about transgender until years later, ze simply considered hirself to be a different kind of male—one who often looked female and who did not mind being referred to as "she" by strangers. Likewise, in Gagné and colleagues' (1997) study of masculine-to-feminine transgender people, the five participants who identified in nonbinary ways (unlike the MTF participants) did not report feeling or wanting to become female as children or teenagers.

The two predominant cultural representations of transgender people have long been the transsexual individual who has transitioned (or is in the process of transitioning) and the ultrafeminine or occasionally ultramasculine cross-dresser. Although vastly different in terms of how they view their identities and how they relate to their bodies, members of both of these groups commonly want to be seen by others simply as female or male. Until recently, there have been few visible images of transgender people who do not present and identify as women or men, and transgender support groups—especially outside of colleges and youth settings—consist largely of female- and/or male-gendered individuals. As a result, people with a nonbinary understanding of their gender have often lacked information, support, and role models, all of which makes it more difficult to adopt a genderqueer identity. "I thought that trans people were all transsexuals," remembers Eric, a twenty-two-year-old interviewee who describes hirself as an "FTM boi." "I didn't know until college that transgender, a more general term, encompassed genderqueers."

In the last decade and a half, genderqueer individuals have been able to see themselves reflected in a growing body of literature, both fictional and nonfictional, that challenges traditional notions of gender and conceptualizes diverse gender possibilities. Five of the fourteen genderqueer interviewees indicated that books about gender or gender theory, most often works by Kate Bornstein and Leslie Feinberg, were instrumental in the process by which they began to see that they need not identify as male or female. "Through those pages, I found community," states Kelly, a white genderqueer interviewee. "As I read, I played around with thinking of myself as trans. . . . I began thinking of myself as a gender-free person." Daniel started considering issues of gender and sexuality in hir late teens, when ze was introduced to "riot grrl" writing and then to academic theorists like Michel Foucault, Eve Kosofsky Sedgwick, Kate Bornstein, and Trinh T. Minh-ha. "Over the course of those years I began to describe my identity roughly as I do now."

Genderqueer individuals face two distinct challenges: being acknowledged in a society that largely comprehends and validates only two gender options; and being recognized as different from other transgender people whose gender identities may be expressed in ways similar to those of genderqueer people. In addition, genderqueer individuals may encounter obstacles if they seek to modify their bodies through hormones or surgery because they may not fit the medical criteria for transitioning, which are often more applicable to the experiences of transsexual than genderqueer individuals. But as more and more people who identify as genderqueer come out publicly, there is likely to be greater public awareness of different forms of gender expression and genderqueer individuals will more readily be seen as distinct from other transgender people—as well as increasingly distinct from each other.

The genderqueer participants expressed their identities in a multitude of ways. Some of the interviewees who had been assigned female at birth were taking hormones and had undergone or were contemplating top surgery. Others chose not to alter their bodies permanently; instead, they modified some of the more visible markers of gender in other ways, such as by breast binding, bodybuilding, having a traditionally male hairstyle, not shaving their body hair, and "packing" (wearing a dildo under their clothing). The genderqueer respondents who had been assigned male at birth likewise changed aspects of themselves that typically indicate gender. Among these changes were growing their hair long, undergoing electrolysis or other techniques to remove facial hair, using makeup and nail polish, and wearing "feminine" earrings and other jewelry.

Clothing and mannerisms were also important ways through which many of the genderqueer participants expressed their gender identity and sought to destabilize traditional gender markers. Some of the interviewees dressed androgynously—wearing non-gender-specific shirts, pants, and shoes—or combined elements of traditionally men's and women's clothing to indicate that they identified as neither, both, or somewhere in between female and male. Other participants, like Eric, completely cross-dressed. Eric combines aspects of lesbian and gay cultures to present as a "gay boi" and buys all of hir clothes from the men's departments at stores. For Zander, a Latino and white participant in hir thirties, changing from a lesbian to a genderqueer identity meant simply changing labels, as ze already wore traditionally male clothing, had short hair, and had a gender-neutral name.

Several interviewees indicated that mannerisms played a significant role in how they sought to present to others as gender ambiguous or nontraditionally gendered. Eric, for example, watches men and women, especially lesbians and gay men, for cues on ways that ze might be read as more "queer." Shannon, a white genderqueer participant in hir thirties, acts in ways that challenge the behavior expected of individuals assigned female at birth, such as by making eye contact with strangers and sitting with hir knees apart. These mannerisms, combined with hir "usually androgynous clothing, hairy legs, small breasts, and shaved head," mean that Shannon frequently receives what ze describes as "that 'Is it a boy or a girl?' look."

ENCOUNTERING RESISTANCE TO A NONBINARY
GENDER EXPRESSION OR IDENTITY

As discussed in chapter 3 and in the literature (e.g., Lombardi et al. 2001), many transgender people—including many genderqueer individuals—have experienced hostility, discrimination, and violence because of their gender identity and/or expression. In the case of genderqueer individuals, genderism often takes the form of opposition to their unwillingness to identify as male or female and to conform to a binary understanding of gender. For example, the few people to whom Esther has disclosed hir gender identity seemed accepting of other transgender people but disapproved of hir as genderqueer, expecting hir to decide between male and female and failing to understand someone who rejects both labels and expresses as male and female at different times.

Shannon has received support for hir identity from the people closest to hir, except from hir mother. Ze states:

> [My mother is] generally really open-minded about my sexuality queerness and attends PFLAG in St. Louis, where she lives and I'm originally from. But when I came out to her as genderqueer, it kind of blew her mind. She accused me of doing too much reading in graduate school, where I was going for an M.A. in Women's Studies and, presumably, was having my mind poisoned by the unrealistic gender notions of radical feminists. . . . She believes that it's natural for there to be only two genders/ sexes. . . . So she rejects out of hand the entire premise that gender is socially constructed, that there can be any division between sex and gender identity (although she accepts my trans aunt—mostly, I think, because my aunt transitioned entirely to the "other side," so her gender identity is still understandable and remains within the comfortable binary), and that any nonbinary gender identity can exist. In short, she thinks I'm incredibly deluded, unrealistic, and out-of-touch with (her) "reality."

Genderqueer respondents who sought to have other people refer to them using a different name or gender-neutral pronouns encountered some of the greatest hostility. The individuals they knew who were antagonistic toward genderqueer identities frequently expressed this disapproval through their unwillingness to use the appropriate, nongendered language, even after being corrected. When 'Ron asked to be called by this name (which is a portion of hir former name) and by gender-neutral pronouns, some people responded derisively, asking with disdain, "*What* am I supposed to call you?" Because ze has struggled to get others to see hir as genderqueer and to stop using hir birth name, 'Ron thinks that ze may change hir name entirely to break with hir gendered past.

Other genderqueer participants did not insist on being known by gender-neutral pronouns or did not constantly correct people who used the wrong pronouns; they found that it required too much effort to convince others to rethink how they conceive of gender and to stop using gendered language. "I haven't been terribly successful in my pronoun desires," Shannon admits. "There are a couple people in my now-former chorus who were great about using them not only for me but as their default gender-neutral pronouns. . . . No one else uses them for me, as far as I can tell." Shannon had to make a conscious effort hirself to become accustomed to gender-neutral pronouns, so ze can empathize with nongenderqueer people who have difficulty using them.

NOT FITTING IN WITH TRANSGENDER OR LGBT COMMUNITIES

The opposition encountered by the genderqueer interviewees frequently came from other transgender people, specifically transsexual women and men, who did not take genderqueer identities seriously and saw it as a fad or phase. Other transsexual individuals viewed the genderqueer respondents as not "transgender enough" because they had often not transitioned completely (or at all). For their part, some of the genderqueer participants did not consider themselves to be transgender because they felt that transgender people frequently reinforce a binary understanding of gender by identifying strictly as male or female and by engaging in stereotypically female or male modes of appearance and behavior.

Given that genderqueer individuals reject dichotomous categories to describe their gender, it is not surprising that most also do not identify their sexual orientation in binary ways. Of the fourteen self-identified genderqueer people interviewed, the vast majority (86 percent) characterized their sexual orientation as queer, bisexual, pansexual, or open. But much as with the reaction they received from other transgender people, many found little or no understanding or acceptance in LGBT communities. The intolerance ranged from genderqueer identities being dismissed as a joke at an LGBT gathering to threats of violence for not conforming to gender and sexual expectations. In one of the more extreme cases, Mary-Lynn, a thirty-eight-year-old white and American Indian (Choctaw) who initially identified as a butch lesbian, was harassed and threatened with assault on several occasions by butch lesbians who felt that ze was violating group norms in hir appearance and behavior. Similar to hir experiences in non-LGBT communities,

Mary-Lynn was repeatedly confronted with the question, "What are you?"

CREATING A HOME WITHIN OR OUTSIDE OF
TRANSGENDER/LGBT COMMUNITIES

Given the perceived lack of support from transgender and LGBT communities, several of the interviewees indicated that they felt isolated. When asked where ze receives support for identifying as genderqueer, Esther replied, "I really don't. There's a LJ [Live Journal] genderqueer community, but most of the people there are androgynous or transgendered. Only a few others have identified as I do." Kelly expressed a similar sentiment. The few people to whom ze has disclosed hir gender identity have been supportive, but most of these individuals live far away from hir. As a result, Kelly feels that ze does not have a local community and is "constantly on guard because [ze doesn't] feel as though that safety net is close by."

Whereas the transsexual and cross-dressing participants typically found a sense of safety and support within transgender and/or LGBT communities, the genderqueer interviewees could not always count on being embraced by other transgender people. Thus, to a greater extent than many of the other respondents, they had to create their own communities. In many cases, these friendship and support networks consisted of individuals who shared their experience being genderqueer. Zander, for example, knew other genderqueer people when ze came out because ze had friends who, like hirself, had moved from identifying as lesbian to identifying as transgender. Eric's biggest supporters are hir partner and hir "best gay boi friend." They help hir with clothes, binding, accessories, hair style, and other parts of hir gender presentation.

Along with the difficulties of finding an established community to which they can belong, some of the genderqueer participants felt isolated by virtue of having to live in a society that largely adheres to a strict gender binary. The respondents who were in college, for example, had to contend with residence hall rooms, locker rooms, bathrooms, sports teams, fraternities and sororities, and certain social traditions that were divided along gender lines; furthermore, they had to choose between marking "male" or "female" when filling out campus forms. Workplaces are generally less gender segregated, but bathrooms (and sometimes locker rooms) often remain an obstacle for people who do not feel safe or comfortable in gender-dichotomous spaces. But as more and more gender-nonconforming youth come out and expect to have their needs addressed by schools and other institutions, policies and practices that had been based on a gender binary are changing to be more inclusive of people of all genders (Transgender Law and Policy Institute 2011a).

SUMMARY OF THE MILESTONES FOR TRANSGENDER PEOPLE

This chapter has examined the similarities and differences in how the study's participants came to identify and accept themselves as transgender. Although the broad categories we use—MTF, FTM, cross-dresser, and genderqueer—do not capture the complexities of all of the ways that transgender people characterize and express their gender identities, these groups represent some of the main components of the transgender "umbrella," and individuals in each group often share common milestones in their processes of identity formation. The various milestones may be experienced differently or not at all by members of a transgender group. In particular, younger transgender people may not experience a delay in identifying and embracing their gender identities given the availability of online resources and the visibility of transgender people in the media and popular culture.

Although there are often differences within a transgender group, often there also are similarities between groups. Regardless of their specific gender identities, transgender people typically feel gender different from a young age and learn to hide these feelings from others for fear of rejection or hostility. Members of all groups sought to gather information about transgender experiences, which included talking with and often meeting others like themselves. Through these interactions, they found role models and came to understand that they could lead happy and healthy lives as transgender people. Some also gained the encouragement they needed to transition, to cross-dress in public, or otherwise begin to challenge gender expectations.

The respondents who cross-dressed only when they were alone could decide if they wanted to tell anyone else about their gender identities. The transgender participants who were transitioning or presenting publicly as a gender different than the one assigned to them at birth had no choice about coming out. The question was not *whether* they should disclose but rather when and how they should do so. All of the interviewees—no matter how they identified as transgender—found that relationships with partners, friends, family members, and coworkers changed after the revelation. Some relationships ended, became more distant, or were strained because the other people could not accept them as transgender. But relationships changed even when others were completely supportive because in some sense the other people had to acquaint themselves with a different person than the one they once knew.

Finally, many of the participants across all gender identities came to embrace themselves as transgender or as having a transgender past. They developed a sense of wholeness even if they could not always express their gender identity publicly, even though they might be recognized by others as having been assigned a different gender at birth, and even when their bodies were different from those of most other women or men. For some, it was a quick and relatively painless process; others spent years in denial and self-hatred before becoming comfortable with themselves and achieving an overall sense of well-being.

Eric

Pauline

Shannon

Tristan

5

TRANSGENDER YOUTH AND IMPLICATIONS FOR HIGHER EDUCATION

I'm not open about [identifying as an androgyny]. I don't even know how to talk about it and the few times I've even brought the discussion up with either straight or gay friends, they look at me like I'm from outer space. It's too far out there on the edge to have any bearing on the mainstay of reality as anyone knows it. There just seems to be no getting around being boxed into familiar categories of male/female, straight/gay/bi.

—LINDA

In this final chapter, we focus on higher education because, as professionals in the field, we see increasing numbers of college students coming out publicly as transgender or as gender nonconforming. Twenty years ago, it was rare to find a student at any college or university who openly identified as transgender. Today, informal and organized transgender groups exist at many institutions; even small colleges, religiously affiliated schools, and military academies report having transgender students on their campuses.

Even so, few colleges and universities have developed comprehensive policies and practices to address the needs of transgender students and acknowledge their experiences. Transgender people are still completely ignored and invisible in most institutional structures; college curricula and cocurricular activities rarely encompass experiences beyond male and female; and most faculty, staff, and student leaders lack training on gender diversity.

As we discuss in this chapter, the campus climates and institutional processes of colleges and universities must be radically changed if higher education is to be truly inclusive of gender-nonconforming students.

IDENTITY FORMATION AMONG TRANSGENDER YOUTH

The results of our survey and the follow-up interviews indicate that transgender youth in the early twenty-first century are often more connected to resources and feel less isolated than the youth who came out as transgender in previous decades. Owing to the Internet and the greater visibility of transgender people in popular culture and the media, most of the participants who were in their late teens and twenties had become aware of transgender people at a younger age than had the older participants. Many also knew other transgender people relatively sooner, having met others online and often subsequently "in real life." Among the approximately 300 individuals we interviewed by e-mail, more than two-thirds of the eighteen- to twenty-two-year-olds had already met other transgender people by the time they began to identify as transgender themselves, as compared with only about one-third of the interviewees in their forties and about one-fourth of those in their fifties and older. In fact, more than half of the older participants did not meet another transgender person until they were at least forty years old.

Because they had known about and met others like themselves from an early age, most of the younger people we interviewed reported that they began to identify as transgender while still teenagers. Obviously, these interviewees must have accepted their gender identity at a young age or else they would not have discovered and wanted to participate in our study. Yet few of the older participants indicated that they had acknowledged being transgender during adolescence, which suggests that these results reflect a shift in transgender identity formation and not merely survey bias.

Most of the individuals we interviewed, regardless of age, recognized themselves as different from other people of their assigned gender as young children, and almost all did so by the end of their teenage years. However, most of the participants who were in their thirties or older had hidden or repressed how they felt for years, if not decades, in the face of opposition (from family members, peers, and societal institutions) and a lack of information, role models, and sources of support. Brianna, a forty-eight-year-old white transsexual woman, spoke for many of the participants when she described feeling that she was living the life that others expected of her:

As a child it is hard to identify as a transsexual when you don't know what a transsexual is. It "felt wrong" to have to play masculine games, sports, wear boy clothes, et cetera. . . . I don't know that I understood why. Later, the "times" and environment I was raised in was not conducive to questioning one's gender and there was no information available about others with the same issues. . . . There were no options available, so I played the role of a male without telling anyone about my issues until I told my spouse around age thirty. In the years after that, I researched and explored my feelings through therapy and support groups until eighteen years later I am finally in transition.

Like a number of the older interviewees, Brianna also commented on the greater availability of transgender resources now than when she was growing up. She concluded that, given the different social and cultural landscape in the early twenty-first century, "[her] experiences are probably no longer a valid representation of what a younger transsexual goes through today."

As Brianna suggested, the interviewees in their late teens and twenties did have a significantly different experience in coming to embrace a transgender identity. Even though transgender people today continue to face high levels of discrimination, verbal harassment, and physical assault, the younger participants typically did not go through an extensive period of denial or concealment. Among the twenty-one interviewees who were between eighteen and twenty-one years old, only four indicated that they repressed their sense of gender difference throughout childhood and adolescence. More common was the experience of interviewees like Rickey, who had identified as male since he was a young child despite other people telling him that he was a girl. In sixth and seventh grade, he learned about the concept of transsexuality by doing some research and was better able then to understand how he felt. Previously, he had believed the stereotype that transgender people are all female-presenting cross-dressers who do not know how to "pass" as women—"men in frilly pink dresses and tacky blonde wigs."

Like many of the older participants, a majority of the traditionally college-aged participants initially adopted some other sexual or gender identity. For example, several of the female-assigned respondents thought of themselves as butch lesbians or as genderqueer individuals before identifying as transsexual men. One person who identified as a transsexual man now describes himself as "somewhere in between," and one young transsexual woman initially believed that she might be an effeminate gay man. Where the younger people differed, though, was in the amount of time spent in their previous identities. Just as few of the eighteen- to twenty-two-year-olds experienced a lengthy period of self-denial, few also maintained their previous identities for very long. Whereas many of the older participants seemed to use other identities as a means to avoid facing their "true selves," sometimes for years or decades, many of the younger participants—who typically had greater access to transgender information and to other transgender people—experimented relatively briefly with different identities before arriving at one that felt right to them.

Martin, an eighteen-year-old FTM individual, was one of the interviewees who "tried out a lot of identities." He came out to himself two-and-a-half years ago as transgender but "wasn't sure what 'type.'" After extensive reading, online research, and talking to other transgender people, he realized a year later that he was a transsexual man and began the process of transitioning. Caiden, a twenty-one-year-old transgender interviewee, initially thought of himself as a lesbian. He "never felt comfortable in that identity, but it was the only language [he] knew." Being from a conservative family in a small town, he had never heard of transgender people until he went to college, where he met a couple of openly transgender students and attended a "Transgender 101" panel. Through these experiences, he discovered a language that could describe how he felt.

THE RESPONSIBILITIES OF COLLEGES AND UNIVERSITIES

With more and more transgender people coming out to themselves and others during childhood or adolescence, many colleges and universities are witnessing a steadily growing number of openly transgender students. These students are expecting to be recognized and to have their needs met by their institutions. However, campuses have been largely unprepared to meet these needs and so now are scrambling to provide support services and to create more inclusive policies and practices. A rapidly increasing number of colleges and universities are adding "gender identity and/or expression" to their nondiscrimination policies; creating gender-inclusive bathrooms, locker rooms, and housing options; providing a means for transgender students who have not legally changed their names or had gender confirmation surgeries to use a preferred name and to change the gender on public records and documents; and covering hormones and surgeries for transitioning students as part of student health insurance. However, more than 90 percent of two- and four-year institutions in the United States have not taken any of these steps and remain completely inaccessible and inhospitable to transgender students (Transgender Law and Policy Institute 2011a, 2011b).

Furthermore, even those colleges and universities that have implemented transgender-supportive policies and practices still remain firmly entrenched in a binary gender system and largely privilege gender-conforming students. In his study of the experiences of transgender students at two large, midwestern public universities that offer some transgender support services, Brent Bilodeau (2009) found that genderism permeated every aspect of campus life: the academic classroom, campus employment and career planning, LGBT and other student organizations and communities, and campus facilities. The student interviewees who identified or expressed their gender outside of a binary had an especially difficult time finding support on their campuses. Even though some progress had been made to recognize and address the needs of transgender people, the overriding assumption governing individual attitudes and institutional structures was that students were either male or female.

Similarly, even though the general campus climate for transgender people has improved during the last decade as transgender students and allies have increasingly organized and sought to educate others, many transgender students indicate that they continue to experience a hostile college environment. A recent study (Dugan, Kusel, & Simounet 2010) compared the experiences of ninety-one transgender-identified students with matched samples of nontransgender lesbian, gay, and bisexual and nontransgender heterosexual students. The researchers found that the transgender students "reported more frequent encounters with harassment and discrimination as well as a significantly lower overall sense of belonging within the campus community" and significantly lower capacities on two educational outcome measures (18).

Colleges and universities can be supportive of transgender students by implementing the transgender-inclusive policies and practices that have been suggested by educators and advocates in the field (Beemyn 2005; Beemyn, Curtis, et al. 2005; Beemyn, Domingue, et al. 2005; Bilodeau 2009). However, the changes needed cannot end there. Having a process whereby students can change the male/female designation on their college records, for example, is of little value to gender-nonconforming students who fit into neither box. Gender-segregated cocurricular activities (e.g., fraternities, sororities, and athletic teams) and "women's" health and support services likewise ignore and exclude the growing number of genderqueer and androgynous students.

Obviously, policies related to participation in intercollegiate sports and fraternities and sororities are beyond the purview of an individual college. But institutions still have the ability to

implement transgender inclusion in other ways, such as through in-
tramural athletics and multigendered fraternities, while advocating
for change on the national level. Similarly, colleges and universities
that use the standard undergraduate admissions form produced by
the Common Application can support efforts by campus LGBT center administrators to expand the "gender" category on the application form to enable transgender and other gender-nonconforming
students to self-identify.

Beyond developing practices and policies throughout the institution that are inclusive and supportive of both transgender and
other gender-nonconforming students, colleges and universities
should establish a no-tolerance policy for anti-transgender harassment and discrimination. Such a policy would be similar to how
institutions have addressed sexual harassment and would involve
development of a formal grievance procedure with clearly defined
penalties and implementation of a mandatory transgender awareness training program for all faculty and staff supervisors. Only after a complete transformation of institutional cultures will colleges
and universities become truly welcoming to transgender students.

THE LIVES OF TRANSGENDER PEOPLE TODAY

In retrospect, what it meant to be transgender was relatively simple
prior to the twenty-first century. Depending on whether they wanted
to transition or not, individuals typically considered themselves to
be either transsexuals or cross-dressers. Today, young people who
are coming out as transgender identify in myriad ways beyond
a gender binary. In our survey, respondents offered more than a
hundred different descriptions for their gender identity besides the
traditional categories of men, women, and transgender; these included "fluid," "neutral," "queer," "two-spirit," "somewhere between transsexual and cross-dresser," "FTM TG stone butch drag
king," and "no easy definition, some other kind of man." Lacking adequate words to describe themselves, some participants gave
percentages (e.g., "49 percent masculine, 51 percent feminine" and
"male 85 percent, cross-dresser 15 percent") or simply said that

there was no language yet available that captured who they were. They were just themselves.

By identifying themselves in multigendered ways, transgender and other gender-nonconforming youth are radically changing the definition of gender and how gender identity will be viewed in the future. Long gone are the days when gender could be limited to the categories of women and men. But so, too, is the time when transgender can be considered a catchall third option, creating a gender "trinary." We live in a world where gender is more complex and more fluid. It is not enough to dispense with the notion of a gender binary; we must embrace and celebrate the idea that gender is bound only by the limits of people's spirits.

APPENDIX A

PURPOSE

Thank you for participating in this confidential survey to assist in the development of a transgender identity model. The results of the survey will provide important information about the experiences of transgender people.

PROCEDURES

You will be asked to complete an online survey. Your participation and responses are confidential. Please answer the questions as openly and honestly as possible. You may skip questions. The survey will take about 20 minutes to complete. You must be 18 years of age or older to participate. Please note that you can choose to withdraw your responses at any time before you submit your answers. The survey results will be submitted directly to a secure server where any computer identification that might identify participants is deleted from the submissions. Any comments provided by participants are also separated at submission so that comments are not attributed to any demographic characteristics. These comments will be analyzed using content analysis and submitted as an appendix to the report. Quotes will also be used throughout the report to give "voice" to the quantitative data.

DISCOMFORTS AND RISKS

There are no risks in participating in this research beyond those experienced in everyday life. Some of the questions are personal and might cause discomfort. In the event that any questions asked are disturbing you may stop the survey at any time. Additional resources may be found at:

Gender Education and Advocacy http://www.gender.org/
FTM International http://www.ftmi.org/
The Trevor Project http://www.thetrevorproject.org/ (24-hour hotline)

BENEFITS

The results of the survey will provide important information about the experiences of transgender people.

STATEMENT OF CONFIDENTIALITY

You will not be asked to provide any identifying information and information you provide on the survey will remain confidential. The Office for Research Protections and the Social Science Institutional Review Board may review records related to this project. In the event of any publication or presentation resulting from the research, no personally identifiable information will be shared. Your confidentiality will be kept to the degree permitted by the technology used (e.g., IP addresses will be stripped when the survey is submitted). No guarantees can be made regarding the interception of data sent via the Internet by any third parties.

VOLUNTARY PARTICIPATION

Participation in this research is voluntary. If you decide to participate, you do not have to answer any questions on the survey that you do not wish to answer. *Individuals will not be identified and only group data will be reported* (e.g., the analysis will include only aggregate data). By completing the survey, your informed consent will be implied. Please note that you can choose to withdraw your responses at any time before you submit your answers. Refusal to take part in this research study will involve no penalty or loss of benefits to participants.

RIGHT TO ASK QUESTIONS

You can ask questions about this research. Contact Susan Rankin at (814) 863-8415 (sxr2@psu.edu) with questions. If you have questions about your rights as a research participant, contact The Pennsylvania State University's Office for Research Protections at (814) 865-1775.

If you agree to take part in this research study and the information outlined above, please click on the "Continue" button below, which indicates your consent to participate in this study. It is recommended that you print this statement for your records, or record the address for this site and keep it for reference.

This informed consent form was reviewed and approved by the Social Science Institutional Review Board (IRB #21490) at The Pennsylvania State University on October 28, 2005. This informed consent form was also reviewed and approved by the Social Science Institutional Review Board (#2005B0270) at The Ohio State University on November 1, 2005.

[Continue button: leads participant to the survey. Respondents who decline to participate are led to a page that thanks them for considering participating in the study.]

DIRECTIONS

- Please read and answer each question carefully, and for each answer, click on the appropriate oval.
- If you want to change an answer, click on the oval of your new answer and your previous response will be erased.
- You may decline to answer specific questions.

SURVEY TERMS AND DEFINITIONS

CLIMATE: Current attitudes, behaviors, and standards of employees and students concerning the level of respect for individual needs, abilities, and potential.

DISABILITY: A physical, cognitive, and/or emotional attribute/ condition that substantially limits one or more major life activities. Some examples include, but are not limited to, blindness, diabetes, learning disabilities, deafness, depression, attention deficit disorder, etc.

GENDER IDENTITY: How one sees oneself as a gendered being, which includes one's sense of self and the image that one presents to the world.

RACIAL IDENTITY: A group of people who share a socially constructed category based on generalized beliefs and/or assumptions about their physical features such as skin color, hair type, shape of eyes, physique, etc.

SEXUAL ORIENTATION: This is inclusive of lesbians (women who are emotionally, physically, and sexually attracted to women), gay men (men who are emotionally, physically, and sexually attracted to men), bisexual people (individuals who are emotionally, physically, and sexually attracted to women and men), and heterosexual people (individuals who are emotionally, physically, and sexually attracted to people of a different gender).

TRANSGENDER: Transgender is used as an umbrella term for anyone who transgresses or blurs traditional gender categories, inclusive of female-to-male and male-to-female transsexuals, cross-dressers, drag queens and kings, genderqueers, gender blenders, two-spirit people, androgyny, and other self-defined gender-variant people.

PART 1. DEMOGRAPHIC INFORMATION

Please keep in mind that we will not report any "group" data for groups that may be small enough to compromise identity. Instead, we will combine the groups to eliminate any potential for identifiable demographic information. Please remember that you do not have to answer any question(s) about which you feel uncomfortable.

1. What was the sex assigned to you at birth?
   o female
   o male
2. What is your gender identity?
   o woman
   o man
   o transgender, please specify _____
   o other (please specify) _____
3. What is your gender expression?
   o feminine
   o masculine
   o transgender, please specify _____
   o other (please specify) _____
4. What is your sexual orientation?
   o bisexual
   o gay
   o lesbian
   o heterosexual

o asexual

o other (please specify) _____

5. What is your age?

    o under 18

    o 18–22

    o 23–32

    o 33–42

    o 43–52

    o 53 and over

6. Do you have a physical attribute that substantially affects a major life activity (such as a disability involving seeing, hearing, walking, etc.)?

    o yes   o no

    If yes, please specify type of attribute: _____

7. Do you have a cognitive or emotional attribute (e.g., learning disability, depression, etc.) that substantially affects a major life activity?

    o yes   o no

    If yes, please specify type of attribute: _____

8. What is your race/ethnicity? (If you are of a multiracial/multiethnic/multicultural identity, mark all that apply.)

    o African/African American/black

    o American Indian (tribal affiliation _____)

    o Alaskan Native

    o Asian/Asian American

    o Latino(a)/Hispanic/Chicano(a)

    o Middle Eastern

    o Pacific Islander

    o Hawaiian Native

    o white/Caucasian

    o other (please specify) _____

9. What is your citizenship status?

    o U.S. citizen, born in the United States

    o U.S. citizen, naturalized

    o permanent resident (immigrant)

    o international (nonpermanent resident)

10. To whom are you most sexually attracted?
    o women
    o men
    o both men and women
    o uncertain

PART 2. TRANSGENDER IDENTITY

11. At about what age did you begin to feel "different" from others?
    o 12 and under
    o 13–19
    o 20–29
    o 30–39
    o 40 and over
12. How did you experience this "difference"? (Mark all that apply.)
    o fearful
    o marginalized
    o angry
    o suicidal
    o comfortable
    o curious
    o other (please specify _____)
13. Please explain how you felt "different."

14. At about what age did you begin to feel uncertain about your gender identity?
    o 12 and under
    o 13–19
    o 20–29
    o 30–39
    o 40 and over

15. What led to this sense of uncertainty?

16. At about what age did you begin to feel that you might be transgender?
    o 12 and under
    o 13–19
    o 20–29
    o 30–39
    o 40 and over
17. How did you react when you first thought that you might be transgender?
    o fearful
    o marginalized
    o angry
    o suicidal
    o comfortable
    o curious
    o other (please specify _____)
18. After self-identifying as transgender, how did you begin to express this identity?

19. At about what age did you first understand that there were a group of people whose gender identity or expression did not coincide with their birth sex?
    o 12 and under
    o 13–19
    o 20–29
    o 30–39
    o 40 and over
20. At about what age did you first meet another transgender person?
    o 12 and under
    o 13–19

o 20–29

o 30–39

o 40 and over

21. What was this experience of meeting another transgender person like for you?

22. When you first began to identify as transgender, how did you manage the societal stigma around being transgender?

23. Place yourself on the following continuum with 5 being out to all of your friends as a transgender person, 4 being out to most of your friends, 3 being out to some friends, 2 being out to only a few close friends, and 1 being totally closeted.

1	2	3	4	5
o	o	o	o	o

24. Place yourself on the following continuum with 5 being out to your nuclear family (e.g., parents and siblings) as a transgender person, 4 being out to most of your family, 3 being out to some family members, 2 being out to only a few family members, and 1 being totally closeted.

1	2	3	4	5
o	o	o	o	o

25. Place yourself on the following continuum with 5 being out to your extended family (e.g., grandparents, aunts, uncles, and cousins) as a transgender person, 4 being out to most of your family, 3 being out to some family members, 2 being out to only a few family members, and 1 being totally closeted.

1	2	3	4	5
o	o	o	o	o

26. Place yourself on the following continuum with 5 being out to everyone professionally as a transgender person, 4 being out to most colleagues, 3 being out to some colleagues, 2 being out to a few colleagues, and 1 being totally closeted.

1	2	3	4	5
o	o	o	o	o

27. If you are open about being transgender to nontransgender people, at about what age did you first begin to disclose to others?
   o 12 and under
   o 13–19
   o 20–29
   o 30–39
   o 40 and over
28. To what extent do you socialize with other transgender people?
   o never
   o rarely
   o sometimes
   o often
   o very often
29. In what context do you socialize with other transgender people? (Mark all that apply.)
   o political activism
   o social activities
   o personal support (e.g., support groups)
   o I don't socialize with other transgender people
   o other (please specify _____)
30. How comfortable are you self-identifying as transgender as compared to when you did not self-identify as transgender?
   o very comfortable
   o comfortable
   o neither comfortable nor uncomfortable
   o uncomfortable
   o very uncomfortable

31. How comfortable is your nuclear family (e.g., parents and siblings) with your self-identifying as transgender?
   o very comfortable
   o comfortable
   o neither comfortable nor uncomfortable
   o uncomfortable
   o very uncomfortable

32. How comfortable is your extended family (e.g., grandparents, aunts, uncles, and cousins) with your self-identifying as transgender?
   o very comfortable
   o comfortable
   o neither comfortable nor uncomfortable
   o uncomfortable
   o very uncomfortable

33. How comfortable are your coworkers/colleagues/peers with your self-identifying as transgender?
   o very comfortable
   o comfortable
   o neither comfortable nor uncomfortable
   o uncomfortable
   o very uncomfortable

34. Overall, how comfortable are you with the climate in your workplace or school for transgender people?

very comfortable	comfortable	unsure	uncomfortable	very uncomfortable
1	2	3	4	5

35. Overall, how comfortable are you with the climate where you live?

very comfortable	comfortable	unsure	uncomfortable	very uncomfortable
1	2	3	4	5

PART 3. TRANSGENDER EXPERIENCES

Within the past year, I have:

36. Feared for my physical safety because of my gender identity or gender expression.

never	rarely	sometimes	often	don't know
1	2	3	4	5

37. Concealed my gender identity or gender expression to avoid intimidation.

never	rarely	sometimes	often	don't know
1	2	3	4	5

38. Avoided disclosing my gender identity or gender expression due to a fear of negative consequences, harassment, or discrimination.

never	rarely	sometimes	often	don't know
1	2	3	4	5

39. Been denied employment or advancement or been paid a lower salary due to my gender identity or gender expression.

o yes   o no   o not applicable   o don't know

40. Been a victim of harassment due to my gender identity or gender expression?

o yes   o no (Skip to question 41.)

    40-1. In what form(s) was this harassment? (Mark all that apply.)
    o derogatory remarks
    o threats to expose your gender identity or gender expression
    o pressure to be silent about your gender identity or gender expression
    o direct or indirect verbal harassment or threats
    o denial of services

o written comments (e.g., anti-LGBT flyers, publications, etc.)
o anti-LGBT graffiti
o threats of physical violence
o had physical property damaged or destroyed
o actual physical assault or injury
o other (please specify) _____

40-2. Where did this harassment occur? (Mark all that apply.)
o in the workplace
o in a public space
o at an LGBT event
o other (please specify) _____

40-3. Who was the source of this harassment? (Mark all that apply.)
o family member
o colleague/coworker
o supervisor/manager/boss
o police
o health care professional
o don't know
o other (please specify) _____

40-4. Please describe your reactions to experiencing this conduct. (Mark all that apply.)
o I felt embarrassed
o I told a friend
o I avoided the person who harassed me
o I ignored it
o I left the situation immediately
o I confronted the harasser at the time
o I confronted the harasser later
o I made a complaint to an appropriate official
o I didn't report it for fear of retaliation
o I didn't know whom to go to
o not described above (please describe your reaction)
_____

41. This survey may have raised a large number of issues for you. If you would like to offer additional thoughts or elaborate on your responses, please use the space below to add your comments. Thank you.

["Thank you" page: respondents are directed to this page after hitting the "submit" button.]

THANK YOU FOR YOUR PARTICIPATION IN THIS SURVEY
Your responses will assist us in understanding the experiences of transgender people. If you are interested in speaking with us further about your experiences, we are inviting survey participants to participate in an open-ended interview that will last approximately 1 hour. The topics that will be covered include your elaborating on your experiences as a transgender person.

You might learn more about yourself by participating in this next phase of the project, and your participation will allow others to hear rarely heard transgender voices and perspectives.

The interview will take about 60 minutes and you must be 18 years of age or older. If you are interested in participating, please contact _____.

Thank you for your consideration.

APPENDIX B

Participant Name:

Participant Contact Information:

Participant Pseudonym:

Date of Interview:

Location of Interview:

DEMOGRAPHIC INFORMATION

What was the sex assigned to you at birth?

What is your gender identity?

What is your gender expression?

If you identify as transsexual:
- Are you taking hormones?
- If so, how long have you been on hormones?
- Have you had any transsexual-related surgeries?
- If so, which surgical procedures?

If you identify as a cross-dresser:
- How long have you cross-dressed?
- In what contexts do you cross-dress/not cross-dress?

If you identify as genderqueer:
- How do you express this identity?

If you identify as some other identity, please describe:

What is your sexual orientation?

To whom are you most sexually attracted?

What is your age?

What is your race/ethnicity?

What is your citizenship status?

Do you have a physical attribute that substantially affects a major life activity?

Do you have a cognitive or emotional attribute that substantially affects a major life activity?

INTERVIEW QUESTIONS

(The blanks are how you particularly identify your gender: man, woman, transsexual man or woman, female or male cross-dresser, drag queen or king, genderqueer, etc.)

1) How long have you identified as _____?

2) Did you first identify as _____ or did you identify as some other gender identity first?

3) Please describe the process by which you began to identify as _____.

4) Did you know other _____ when you began to identify as _____?

4a) If so, how did you meet them?

4b) If not, how did you learn about a _____ identity?

5) If you are open to others about being _____, how have these individuals responded to the disclosure?

6) If you are not seen by others as strictly male/female, where do you receive support for identifying as _____?

APPENDIX C

REVIEW OF STATISTICAL ANALYSES

CHAPTER 1: DEMOGRAPHICS OF THE SURVEY PARTICIPANTS

A multivariate analysis of variance (MANOVA), analysis of variance (ANOVA), and binary logistic regression were used to examine whether differences existed between groups with respect to when they began to understand their identity as transgender (see table C.1); for this, we analyzed responses to the following two questions: "What was the sex assigned to you at birth?" and "What is your gender identity?" Instead of separate ANOVAs, we used MANOVAs to analyze the group of age-related questions (as well as questions 23–26) to control for experiment-wise errors stemming from dependent variables that are correlated with each other. Because the variance was not homogeneous, Dunnett's T3 test was employed to compare means of different groups. Based on this analysis, participants were placed into one of four categories: female-to-different-gender (FTDG), male-to-different-gender (MTDG), male-to-female/transgender (MTF/T), and female-to-male/transgender (FTM/T).

For the age questions (table C.1), the participants could select one of the following age groups.

Group 1: 12 and under (except for question 5)
Group 2: 13–19
Group 3: 20–29
Group 4: 30–39
Group 5: 40 and over

Table C.2 gives the average age group and standard deviation on the age questions for each of the transgender groups. After conducting a MANOVA, the existence of a difference among the transgender groups was determined at an alpha of .05 with an $F(28, 9026)$ equal to 27.802 and a p-value of less than .0001 (table C.3).

TABLE C.1   Age questions

	Question
Q5	What is your age at the time of this survey?
Q11	At about what age did you begin to feel "different" from others?
Q14	At about what age did you begin to feel uncertain about your gender identity?
Q16	At about what age did you begin to feel that you might be transgender?
Q19	At about what age did you first understand that there were a group of people whose gender identity or expression did not coincide with their birth sex?
Q20	At about what age did you first meet another transgender person?
Q27	If you are open about being transgender to nontransgender people, at about what age did this occur?

TABLE C.2 Means and standard deviations for age questions

	FTDG		MTDG		MTF/T		FTM/T	
Question	Mean	SD	Mean	SD	Mean	SD	Mean	SD
Q5	2.087	0.147	3.784	0.130	3.816	0.032	2.516	0.055
Q11	1.232	0.069	1.239	0.061	1.177	0.015	1.155	0.026
Q14	1.812	0.126	1.545	0.112	1.680	0.027	1.698	0.047
Q16	2.493	0.150	2.523	0.133	2.561	0.033	2.594	0.056
Q19	2.319	0.131	2.500	0.116	2.833	0.029	2.398	0.049
Q20	2.652	0.125	3.625	0.111	3.656	0.027	2.811	0.047
Q27	2.986	0.124	3.136	0.110	4.119	0.027	3.243	0.046

TABLE C.3 Univariate statistics for age questions

	F-statistic	Degrees of Freedom	p-value	Adjusted R^2
Q5	149.20	(4, 2264)	< .0001	.207
Q11	11.25	(4, 2264)	< .0001	.018
Q14	8.30	(4, 2264)	< .0001	.013
Q16	1.79	(4, 2264)	.128	.001
Q19	18.35	(4, 2264)	< .0001	.030
Q20	72.17	(4, 2264)	< .0001	.112
Q27	83.08	(4, 2264)	< .0001	.126

CHAPTER 2: EXPERIENCES OF TRANSGENDER IDENTITY

TABLE C.4 When respondents felt different (columns) by age group (rows)

		12 and Under	13–19	20–29	30–39	40 and Over	Missing	Total
18 and under	n	242	82	3	0	0	3	330
	%	73.3	24.8	0.9	0.0	0.0	0.9	100.0
Other ages	n	2,483	353	53	19	31	15	2,954
	%	84.1	11.9	1.8	0.6	1.0	0.5	100.0
53 and over	n	131	26	3	2	7	4	173
	%	75.7	15.0	1.7	1.2	4.0	2.3	100.0
Total	n	2,856	461	59	21	38	22	3,457
	%	82.6	13.3	1.7	0.6	1.1	0.6	100.0

TABLE C.5 Significance tests for results reported in table C.4

Test	Value	Degrees of Freedom	Asymptotic Significance (2-sided)
Pearson chi-square	73.041	10	.000
Likelihood ratio	63.608	10	.000

The binary regression coefficients and associated odds ratios are displayed in table C.6 and table C.7. The MTDG and MTF/T groups were less likely to feel marginalized, angry, or suicidal and more likely to feel curious than the FTM/T groups ($p < .001$). The only significant difference (alpha = .05) between the FTM/T and FTDG group was curiosity, where the latter group was more curious.

Based on question 19 ("At about what age did you first understand that there were a group of people whose gender identity or expression did not coincide with their birth sex?"), we found that the MTF/T participants were significantly older than the FTDG and FTM/T participants. The MTDG group was not significantly different from any of the other groups in terms of age.

We used ANOVA to examine the difference in the extent that each group socialized with other transgender people (question 28), which respondents answered on a five-point Likert scale. The average response and standard deviation for each group are shown in table C.11. With an $F(4, 3063)$ equal to 11.03 ($p < .001$), a significant difference existed among the groups at an alpha of .05. Results of the post hoc tests (Tukey's) showed that the MTDG respondents are less likely to socialize with other transgender people than are the FTDG, FTM/T, and MTF/T respondents at an alpha of .05. The ANOVA analysis is in line with the binary logistic regression analysis performed on question 29 (tables C.12 and C.13), which revealed that the MTDG group was less likely to participate in political activism, personal support, and social activities—as well as less likely to socialize with other transgender people—than was the FTM/T group. The MTF/T group was less likely to participate in political activism and social activities and also less likely to socialize with other transgender people than was the FTM/T group.

TABLE C.6 Responses to question 12 ("How did you experience this [sense of] 'difference' from others?") by transgender group (first three choices)

Group	Fearful					Marginalized					Angry				
	B	SE	Wald	p-value	Odds Ratio	B	SE	Wald	p-value	Odds Ratio	B	SE	Wald	p-value	Odds Ratio
FTDG	-0.250	0.230	1.21	.271	0.78	0.11	0.23	0.22	.636	1.11	-0.32	0.233	1.86	.173	0.73
MTDG	0.238	0.188	1.60	.206	1.27	-0.85	0.20	17.58	< .001	0.43	-1.39	0.243	32.78	< .001	0.25
MTF/T	0.150	0.094	2.52	.112	1.16	-0.81	0.10	69.95	< .001	0.45	-1.27	0.102	154.50	< .001	0.28

Note: For all coefficients reported in this table, df = 1.

TABLE C.7 Responses to question 12 ("How did you experience this [sense of] 'difference' from others?") by transgender group (next three choices)

Group	Suicidal					Comfortable					Curious				
	B	SE	Wald	p-value	Odds Ratio	B	SE	Wald	p-value	Odds Ratio	B	SE	Wald	p-value	Odds Ratio
FTDG	0.02	0.24	0.01	.941	1.01	0.20	0.27	0.54	.461	1.22	0.49	0.23	4.60	.032	1.63
MTDG	-1.24	0.27	21.70	< .001	0.29	-0.39	0.27	2.12	.146	0.68	0.92	0.20	22.03	< .001	2.50
MTF/T	-0.94	0.11	77.22	< .001	0.39	-0.25	0.12	4.18	.041	0.78	0.40	0.10	17.85	< .001	1.49

Note: For all coefficients reported in this table, df = 1.

TABLE C.8 Mean and standard deviation on age questions by transgender group

Group	Mean	SD
FTDG	2.319	0.131
MTDG	2.500	0.116
MTF/T	2.833	0.029
FTM/T	2.398	0.049

TABLE C.9 Univariate statistics for question 19 ("At about what age did you first understand that there were a group of people whose gender identity or expression did not coincide with their birth sex?")

F-statistic	Degrees of Freedom	p-value	Adjusted R^2
18.35	(4, 2264)	< .0001	.030

TABLE C.10 Summary of responses to question 29 ("In what context do you socialize with other transgender people?")

Response	Comment
Political activism	MTDG and MTF/T were less likely to be politically active with other transgender than were FTM/T ($p < .01$) FTDG were more likely to be politically active with other transgender than were FTM/T ($p = .05$)
Social activities	MTDG and MTF/T were less likely to be socially active with other transgender than were FTM/T ($p < .01$)
Personal support	FTDG and MTDG were likely to have less personal support with other transgender than were FTM/T ($p < .02$) MTF/T were likely to have more personal support with other transgender than were FTM/T ($p = .025$)
Don't socialize	MTDG and MTF/T were less likely to socialize with other transgender than were FTM/T ($p < .01$)

However, MTF/T respondents were more likely to participate in personal support groups with other transgender people than were the FTM/T participants. The FTDG group was more likely to participate in political activism activities but less likely to participate in personal support groups than the FTM/T group.

TABLE C.11 Mean and standard deviation for question 28 ("To what extent do you socialize with other transgender people?") by transgender group

Group	Mean	SD
FTDG	3.23	1.10
MTDG	2.89	1.20
MTF/T	3.08	1.16
FTM/T	3.23	1.10

TABLE C.12 Responses to question 29 ("In what context do you socialize with other transgender people?") by transgender group (first two choices)

	Political Activism					Social Activities				
Group	B	SE	Wald	p-value	Odds Ratio	B	SE	Wald	p-value	Odds Ratio
FTDG	0.44	0.23	3.84	.050	1.56	−0.19	0.24	0.62	.43	0.83
MTDG	−0.58	0.21	7.69	.006	0.56	−0.63	0.19	10.63	.001	0.53
MTF/T	−0.70	0.10	49.15	< .001	0.50	−0.41	0.10	16.31	< .001	0.66

Note: For all coefficients reported in this table, df = 1.

TABLE C.13 Responses to question 29 ("In what context do you socialize with other transgender people?") by transgender group (next two choices)

	Personal Support					Do Not Socialize				
Group	B	SE	Wald	p-value	Odds Ratio	B	SE	Wald	p-value	Odds Ratio
FTDG	−0.55	0.23	5.66	.017	0.57	0.22	0.43	0.25	.614	1.24
MTDG	−0.51	0.19	7.18	.007	0.60	1.01	0.29	12.40	< .001	2.75
MTF/T	0.21	0.10	5.01	.025	1.24	0.57	0.19	9.61	.002	1.78

Note: For all coefficients reported in this table, df = 1.

When reviewing the data by transgender group, 47 percent (49) of the FTDG participants experienced harassment as compared with 22 percent (33) of the MTDG participants, 27 percent (584) of the MTF/T participants, and 35 percent (231) of the FTM/T participants. Chi-square analysis indicates that this finding is significant and that all differences reported in this section are also significant.

Among the individuals surveyed, a significantly larger percentage of the transgender people of color than transgender white people (33 versus 27 percent) reported experiencing harassment in the previous year because of their gender identity/expression.

TABLE C.14 Affirmative responses to question 40 ("Within the past year, I have been the victim of harassment due to my gender identity or gender expression") by transgender group

Group		
FTDG	n	49
	%	47.1
MTDG	n	33
	%	21.7
MTF/T	n	584
	%	26.8
FTM/T	n	231
	%	35.4

TABLE C.15 Significance tests for results reported in table C.14

Test	Value	Degrees of Freedom	Asymptotic Significance (2-sided)
Pearson chi-square	2.414×10^2	8	.000
Likelihood ratio	166.207	8	.000
Linear-by-linear association	0.612	1	.434

TABLE C.16 Affirmative responses to question 40 ("Within the past year, I have been a victim of harassment due to my gender identity or gender expression?") by race/ethnicity

Race/Ethnicity		
White people	n	808
	%	26.9
People of color	n	138
	%	32.7

TABLE C.17 Significance tests for results reported in table C.16

Test	Value	Degrees of Freedom	Asymptotic Significance (2-sided)
Pearson chi-square	3.904×10^2	4	.000
Likelihood ratio	94.735	4	.000
Linear-by-linear association	0.706	1	.401

TABLE C.18 Basis of gender-motivated physical assault by race/ethnicity

Race/Ethnicity		
White people	n	60
	%	7.4
People of color	n	18
	%	13.0

A significantly higher incidence of physical assault was reported by transgender people of color than by transgender white respondents. The transgender people of color (58 percent, 244 respondents) were significantly more fearful for their safety based on their gender identity/expression than were the transgender white people (49 percent, 1,515 respondents).

Finally, 25 percent (99) of the people of color stated that they had sometimes or often been denied employment, advancement, or a raise because of their gender identity/expression, as compared with 16 percent (469) of the white people.

TABLE C.19 Significance tests for results reported in table C.18

Test	Value	Degrees of Freedom	Asymptotic Significance (2-sided)
Pearson chi-square	7.116	2	.029
Likelihood ratio	5.991	2	.050
Linear-by-linear association	2.710	1	.100

TABLE C.20 Responses to question 36 ("Within the past year, I have feared for my physical safety because of my gender identity or gender expression") by race/ethnicity

Race/Ethnicity		Never	Rarely	Sometimes	Often	Don't Know
White people	n	557	818	1,140	375	67
	%	18.5	27.2	37.9	12.5	2.2
People of color	n	61	96	163	81	15
	%	14.5	22.7	38.6	19.2	3.6

TABLE C.21 Significance tests for results reported in table C.20

Test	Value	Degrees of Freedom	Asymptotic Significance (2-sided)
Pearson chi-square	3.389×10^2	10	.000
Likelihood ratio	109.560	10	.000
Linear-by-linear association	31.812	1	.000

TABLE C.22 Responses to question 39 ("Within the past year, I have been denied employment or advancement or been paid a lower salary due to my gender identity or gender expression") by race/ethnicity

Race/Ethnicity		Never	Rarely or Sometimes	Often
White people	n	1,520	439	274
	%	52.6	15.2	9.5
People of color	n	174	85	59
	%	43.5	21.2	14.8

TABLE C.23 Significance tests for results reported in table C.22

Test	Value	Degrees of Freedom	Asymptotic Significance (2-sided)
Pearson chi-square	30.950	6	.000
Likelihood ratio	29.606	6	.000
Linear-by-linear association	0.503	1	.478

NOTES

Foreword

1. Doe v. Yunits, 2000 WL 33162199 (Mass. Super. 2000).

Introduction

1. The quotes used throughout the book are excerpts from the interviews conducted for this project. The names are the individual's given or adopted name (used with permission of the individual) or a pseudonym (as requested by the individual). In instances where more than one interviewee had the same first name, the first initial of their last names are also used.

2. "Ze" is a gender-neutral pronoun used in place of "she" and "he" and sometimes also "her" and "him" (other people use "sie" for "she"/"he" and "hir" for "her"/"him"). In order to value the individual voices of the participants in our study, we employ the pronouns that they have chosen to use.

3. "Cisgender" is a term for people who are nontransgender; it refers here to individuals whose gender assigned at birth has always

coincided with their gender identity/expression. The prefix "cis" is Latin for "on the same side as," which makes it the antonym of "trans" ("on the opposite side of"). According to historian Susan Stryker, the basis of the words "cisgender" and "cissexual" (nontranssexual individuals) "is to resist the way that 'woman' or 'man' can mean 'nontransgendered woman' or 'nontransgendered man' by default, unless the person's transgender status is explicitly named; it's the same logic that would lead somebody to prefer saying 'white woman' and 'black woman' rather than simply using 'woman' to describe a white woman (thus presenting white as the norm) and 'black woman' to indicate a deviation from the norm" (Stryker 2008:22). See also Fausto-Sterling (2000), Gorton, Buth, & Spade (2005), Green (2006), and Transsexual Roadmap (2010).

4. The purpose of the mixed methods design is to "use qualitative results to assist in explaining and interpreting the findings of a primarily quantitative study" (Creswell 2008:21). Mixed methods designs are appropriate when researchers want to generalize the findings of a population before developing a more detailed view of a complex construct. By using a mixed methods design for such assessment, it is possible to "capture the best of both quantitative and qualitative approaches" (Creswell 2008:22). The mixed methods research is discussed more thoroughly in Johnson and Onwuegbuzie (2004).

5. A more detailed description of these analyses is provided in appendix C.

Chapter 1

1. "Disorders of sex development" is a general term used to describe a variety of intersex conditions in which a person is born with chromosomes, a reproductive system, or a sexual anatomy that is not considered "standard" for either male or female. For more information, see the website of the Accord Alliance: www.accordalliance.org.

2. The definitions offered here will be used throughout the book, but we also agree with Kate Bornstein that terminology is neither definitive nor determined—that it is a starting rather than an ending point. As she states, "definitions have their uses in the same way that road signs make it easy to travel: they point out the directions. But you don't get where you're going when you just stand underneath some

sign, waiting for it to tell you what to do" (Bornstein 1994:21). Insightful discussions of terminology are also provided by Lev (2004) and Stryker (2008).

3. According to the Sapir-Whorf hypothesis, "people perceive the world through the cultural lens of language" (Sapir 1949:162). Thus, language shapes our reality, is a powerful tool of culture, and maintains a system of inequality. Julia Wood (1997) uses the assertions of philosopher Ernst Cassirer (1978) to illustrate how language is used to indicate cultural values and views of women and men, thereby maintaining inequality.

4. For this project, the following were considered to be "people of color" identities: African/African American/black, Alaskan Native, American Indian, Asian/Asian American, Hawaiian Native, Latino(a)/ Hispanic/Chicano(a), Middle Eastern, and Pacific Islander. Although we recognize the vastly different experiences of people of various racial identities (e.g., American Indians versus African Americans) and even within the same racial identity (e.g., Hmong versus Chinese), we collapsed our categories into "people of color" and "white" for much of the analysis because there were so few participants in the different "people of color" categories. The percentages given are based on all of the survey respondents (3,509 people).

Chapter 2

1. "Mahu" is a precolonial Hawaiian word for indigenous people who lived cross-gendered lives.

Chapter 3

1. For a more detailed explanation of the rationale behind and the means of assessing campus climate, see Rankin and Reason (forthcoming).

2. There is sparse research examining the campus climate specifically for transgender people. Most of the research considers both sexual identity and gender identity. This review will focus on the results for transgender communities.

3. Violence motivated or aggravated by hatred or bias is characterized as a hate crime (Lawrence 1999). These acts are far reaching and

affect more than just the person who experienced the hate crime; they also serve to send a "message of intimidation to an entire community of people" (United States House of Representatives, Subcommittee on Crime and Criminal Justice Bias Crimes; cited in Ferber, Grattet, & Jenness 1999:47). See also Haider-Markel (1998).

4. Federal Bureau of Investigation, *Crime in the United States*, 2004. Available at http://www.fbi.gov/about-us/cjis/ucr/crime-in-the-u.s/2004

Chapter 4

1. We did not obtain a large enough sample of male-presenting cross-dressers to examine their experiences separately.

2. Quoted in *Gay Guitarists Worldwide* (2006, June). Retrieved from http://launch.groups.yahoo.com/group/gayguitarists

3. A *cohort* effect is "any effect associated with being a member of a group born at roughly the same time and bonded by common life experiences (e.g., growing up in the 1980s)." *A Dictionary of Business and Management*, Oxford University Press (2006, January). Retrieved from http://www.encyclopedia.com/doc/1O18-cohorteffect.html

REFERENCES

American Psychiatric Association. (1980). *Diagnostic and statistical manual of mental disorders* (3rd ed.). Washington, DC: Author.

American Psychiatric Association. (1987). *Diagnostic and statistical manual of mental disorders* (3rd ed., revised). Washington, DC: Author.

American Psychiatric Association. (1994). *Diagnostic and statistical manual of mental disorders* (4th ed.). Washington, DC: Author.

American Psychiatric Association. (2000). *Diagnostic and statistical manual of mental disorders* (4th ed., text revision). Washington, DC: Author.

American Psychiatric Association. (2010). *Proposed draft revisions to DSM disorders and criteria.* Retrieved August 24, 2010, from http://www.dsm5.org

American Psychological Association. (2010). *Sexual orientation and homosexuality.* Retrieved August 24, 2010, from http://www.apa.org/helpcenter/sexual-orientation.aspx

Baer, M., & Frese, M. (2003). Innovation is not enough: Climate for initiative and psychological safety, process innovations, and firm performance. *Journal of Organizational Behavior, 24,* 45–68.

Bailey, J. M. (2003). *The man who would be queen: The science of gender-bending and transsexualism*. Washington, DC: Joseph Henry Press.

Battle, J., Cohen, C., Fergerson, G., & Audam, S. (2002). *Say it loud, I am black and proud*. Washington, DC: National Gay and Lesbian Policy Institute.

Baumbach, J., & Turner, L. A. (1992). Female gender disorder: A new model and clinical applications. *Journal of Psychology and Human Sexuality, 5*(4), 107–129.

Baumeister, R. F. (2000). Gender differences in erotic plasticity: The female sex drive as socially flexible and responsive. *Psychological Bulletin, 126*, 347–374.

Beam, C. (2007). *Transparent: Love, family, and living the T with transgender teenagers*. Orlando, FL: Harcourt.

Beemyn, B. G. (2003). Serving the needs of transgender college students. *Journal of Gay and Lesbian Issues in Education, 1*(1), 33–50.

Beemyn, B. G. (2005). Making campuses more inclusive of transgender students. *Journal of Gay and Lesbian Issues in Education, 3*(1), 77–89.

Beemyn, B. G. (2008). Genderqueer. In C. J. Summers (Ed.), *glbtq: An encyclopedia of gay, lesbian, bisexual, transgender, and queer culture*. Retrieved August 24, 2010, from www.glbtq.com/social-sciences/genderqueer.html

Beemyn, B. G., Curtis, B., Davis, M., & Tubbs, N. J. (2005). Transgender issues on college campuses. In R. L. Sanlo (Ed.), *Gender identity and sexual orientation: Research, policy, and personal perspectives* (pp. 41–49). San Francisco: Jossey-Bass.

Beemyn, B. G., Domingue, A., Pettitt, J., & Smith, T. (2005). Suggested steps to make campuses more trans-inclusive. *Journal of Gay and Lesbian Issues in Education, 3*(1), 89–104.

Benjamin, H. (1966). *The transsexual phenomenon*. New York: Julian Press.

Bensimon, E. M. (2004). The diversity scorecard: A learning approach to institutional change. *Change, 36*(1), 45–52.

Berry, P., McGuffee, K., Rush, J., & Columbus, S. (2003). Discrimination in the workplace: The firing of a transsexual. *Journal of Human Behavior in the Social Environment, 8*(2/3), 225–239.

Bilodeau, B. (2009). *Genderism: Transgender students, binary systems and higher education*. Saarbrücken, Germany: Verlag Dr. Müller.

Blackless, M., Charuvastra, A., Derryck, A., Fausto-Sterling, A., Lauzanne, K., & Lee, E. (2000). How sexually dimorphic are we? Review and synthesis. *American Journal of Human Biology, 12*, 151–166.

Blanchard, R. (2000). *Autogynephilia and the taxonomy of gender identity disorders in biological males.* Paper presented at the International Academy of Sex Research. Retrieved August 24, 2010, from www.autogynephilia.org/ColoredParisTalk_files/v3_document.htm

Bolin, A. (1988). *In search of Eve: Transsexual rites of passage.* South Hadley, MA: Bergin & Garvey.

Bolin, A. (1994). Transcending and transgendering: Male-to-female transsexuals, dichotomy and diversity. In G. Herdt (Ed.), *Third sex, third gender: Beyond sexual dimorphism in culture and history* (pp. 447–485). New York: Zone Books.

Bornstein, K. (1994). *Gender outlaw: On men, women, and the rest of us.* New York: Routledge.

Brill, S., & Pepper, R. (2008). *The transgender child: A handbook for families and professionals.* San Francisco: Cleis Press.

Brown, G. R. (1988). Transsexuals in the military: Flight into hypermasculinity. *Archives of Sexual Behavior, 17*(6), 527–537.

Brown, R. D., Clarke, B., Gortmaker, V., & Robinson-Keilig, R. (2004). Assessing the campus climate for gay, lesbian, bisexual, and transgender (GLBT) students using a multiple perspectives approach. *Journal of College Student Development, 45*, 8–26.

Buhrich, N., & Beaumont, T. (1981). Comparison of transvestism in Australia and America. *Archives of Sexual Behavior, 10*(3), 269–279.

Buhrich, N., & McConaghy, N. (1977). The discrete syndromes of transvestism and transsexualism. *Archives of Sexual Behavior, 6*(6), 483–495.

Buhrich, N., & McConaghy, N. (1978). Parental relationships during childhood in homosexuality, transvestism and transsexualism. *Australian and New Zealand Journal of Psychiatry, 12*, 103–108.

Buhrich, N., & McConaghy, N. (1979). Tests of gender feelings and behavior in homosexuality, transvestism and transsexualism. *Journal of Clinical Psychology, 35*(1), 187–191.

Bullough, B., & Bullough, V. (1993). *Cross dressing, sex, and gender.* Philadelphia: University of Pennsylvania Press.

Bullough, B., & Bullough, V. (1997). Men who cross-dress: A survey. In B. Bullough, V. L. Bullough, & J. Elias (Eds.), *Gender blending* (pp. 174–188). Amherst, NY: Prometheus Books.

Bullough, V., Bullough, B., & Smith, R. (1983). A comparative study of male transvestites, male to female transsexuals, and male homosexuals. *Journal of Sex Research, 19*(3), 238–257.

Butler, J. (1990). *Gender trouble: Feminism and the subversion of identity.* New York: Routledge.

Butler, J. (2004). *Undoing gender.* New York: Routledge.

Cameron, D. (2005). Language, gender, and sexuality: Current issues and new directions. *Applied Linguistics, 26*(4), 482–502.

Caroll, J. L., & Wolpe, P. R. (1996). *Sexuality and gender in society.* New York: Harper-Collins.

Cass, V. C. (1979). Homosexual identity formation: A theoretical model. *Journal of Homosexuality, 4,* 219–235.

Cassirer, E. (1978). *An essay on man.* New Haven, CT: Yale University Press.

Clements-Nolle, K., Marx, R., & Katz, M. (2006). Attempted suicide among transgender persons: The influence of gender-based discrimination and victimization. *Journal of Homosexuality, 51*(3), 53–69.

Confucius. (1980). Rectification of names. In J. R. Ware (Trans.), *The analects of Confucius* (book 13, verse 3). Retrieved August 24, 2010, from http://www.analects-ink.com/mission/Confucius_Rectification.html

Creswell, J. (2008). *Research design: Qualitative, quantitative, and mixed methods approaches* (3rd ed.). Thousand Oaks, CA: Sage.

Cromwell, J. (1999). *Transmen and FTMs: Identities, bodies, genders, and sexualities.* Urbana: University of Illinois Press.

Daley, C., Kulger, E., & Hirshman, J. (2000). *Walking while transgender: Law enforcement harassment of San Francisco's transgender/transsexual community.* San Francisco: Ella Baker Center for Human Rights/TransAction.

D'Augelli, A. R. (1994a). Identity development and sexual orientation: Toward a model of lesbian, gay, and bisexual development. In E. J. Trickett, R. J. Watts, & D. Birman (Eds.), *Human diversity: Perspectives on people in context* (pp. 312–333). San Francisco: Jossey-Bass.

D'Augelli, A. R. (1994b). Lesbian and gay male development: Steps toward an analysis of lesbian and gay men's lives. In B. Greene

& G. M. Herek (Eds.), *Lesbian and gay psychology: Theory, research, and clinical applications* (pp. 118–132). Beverly Hills, CA: Sage.

Denny, D. (2006). Transgender communities of the United States in the late twentieth century. In P. Currah, R. M. Juang, & S. P. Minter (Eds.), *Transgender rights* (pp. 171–191). Minneapolis: University of Minnesota Press.

Devor, A. H. (1997a). *FTM: Female-to-male transsexuals in society.* Bloomington: Indiana University Press.

Devor, A. H. (1997b). More than manly women: How female-to-male transsexuals reject lesbian identities. In B. Bullough, V. L. Bullough, & J. Elias (Eds.), *Gender blending* (pp. 87–102). Amherst, NY: Prometheus Books.

Devor, A. H. (2004a). Witnessing and mirroring: A fourteen stage model of transsexual identity formation. In U. Leli & J. Drescher (Eds.), *Transgender subjectivities: A clinician's guide* (pp. 41–67). Binghamton, NY: Haworth Medical Press.

Devor, A. H. (2004b). Witnessing and mirroring: A fourteen stage model of transsexual identity formation. *Journal of Gay & Lesbian Psychotherapy, 8,* 41–67.

Diamond, L. M., & Savin-Williams, R. C. (2003). Explaining diversity in the development of same-sex sexuality among young women. In L. D. Garnets & D. C. Kimmel (Eds.), *Psychological perspectives on lesbian, gay, and bisexual experiences* (2nd ed., pp. 130–148). New York: Columbia University Press.

Diamond, M. (Ed.). (2004). *From the inside out: Radical gender transformation, FTM and beyond.* San Francisco: Manic D Press.

Docter, R. F. (1988). *Transvestites and transsexuals: Toward a theory of cross-gender behavior.* New York: Plenum Press.

Docter, R. F., & Fleming, J. S. (1993). Dimensions of transvestism and transsexualism: The validation and factorial structure of the cross-gender questionnaire. *Journal of Psychology and Human Sexuality, 5,* 15–37.

Docter, R. F., & Prince, V. (1997). Transvestism: A survey of 1032 cross-dressers. *Archives of Sexual Behavior, 26*(6), 589–605.

Dugan, J. P., Kusel, M. L., & Simounet, D. (2010). *Transgender college students: An exploratory study of perceptions, engagement, and educational outcomes.* Paper presented at the American College Personnel Association Convention.

Ebaugh, H. R. F. (1988). *Becoming an ex: The process of role exit.* Chicago: University of Chicago Press.

Ekins, R. (1997). *Male femaling: A grounded theory approach to cross-dressing and sex changing.* New York: Routledge.

Eliason, M. J. (1996). Identity formation for lesbian, bisexual, and gay persons: Beyond a "minoritizing" view. *Journal of Homosexuality, 30*(3), 31–58.

Elshtain, J. B. (1998). Contemporary directions in liberal feminism. In R. Tong (Ed.), *Feminist thought* (pp. 87–93). Boulder, CO: Westview Press.

Erhardt, V. (2007). *Head over heels: Wives who stay with cross-dressers and transsexuals.* New York: Haworth Press.

Ettner, R. (1999). *Gender loving care: A guide to counseling gender-variant clients.* New York: Norton.

Evans, N. J., & Broido, E. (1999). Coming out in college residence halls: Negotiation, meaning making, challenges, supports. *Journal of College Student Development, 40,* 658–668.

Fausto-Sterling, A. (1993, March/April). The five sexes: Why male and female are not enough. *The Sciences,* 20–24.

Fausto-Sterling, A. (2000). *Sexing the body.* New York: Basic Books.

Federal Bureau of Investigation. *Crime in the United States, 2004.* Retrieved April 24, 2011, from http://www.fbi.gov/about-us/cjis/ucr/crime-in-the-u.s/2004

Feinberg, L. (1998). *Trans liberation: Beyond pink or blue.* Boston: Beacon Press.

Felsenthal, K. D. (2004). Enacting masculinity. Antigay violence and group rape as a participatory theater. *Sexuality Research & Social Policy: Journal of NSRC, 1*(2), 25–40.

Ferber, A. L., Grattet, R., & Jenness, V. (1999). *Hate crimes in America: What do we know?* Washington, DC: American Sociological Association.

Freund, K., Steiner, B. W., & Chan, S. (1982). Two types of cross gender identity. *Archives of Sexual Behavior, 11,* 49–63.

Gagné, P., Tewksbury, R., & McGaughey, D. (1997). Coming out and crossing over: Identity formation and proclamation in a transgender community. *Gender & Society, 11*(4), 478–508.

Gehi, P. S., & Arkles, G. (2007). Unraveling injustice: Race and class impact of Medicaid exclusions of transition-related health care for transgender people. *Journal of Sexual Research and Social Policy,* 4, 7–35.

GenderPAC. (1997). *The first national survey of transgender violence.* Washington, DC: Author.

GenderPAC. (2006). *50 under 30: Masculinity and the war on American youth.* Washington, DC: Author.

GID Reform Advocates. (2004). *GID reform advocates: Because our identities are not disordered.* Retrieved August 24, 2010, from http://www.transgender.org/gidr/index.html

Girshick, L. B. (2008). *Transgender voices: Beyond women and men.* Hanover, NH: University Press of New England.

Glaser, B. G., & Strauss, A. L. (1967). *The discovery of grounded theory: Strategies for qualitative research.* New York: de Gruyter.

Glick, W. H. (1985). Conceptualizing and measuring organizational and psychological climate: Pitfalls of multilevel research. *Academy of Management Review, 10*(3), 601–616.

Gorton, R., Buth, J., & Spade, D. (2005). *Medical therapy and health maintenance for transgender men: A guide for health care providers.* San Francisco: Lyon-Martin Women's Health Services.

Green, E. R. (2006). Debating trans inclusion in the feminist movement: A trans-positive analysis. *Journal of Lesbian Studies, 10*(1/2), 231–248.

Green, J. (2004). *Becoming a visible man.* Nashville, TN: Vanderbilt University Press.

Greenberg, J. A. (2006). *The roads less traveled: The problem with sex categories.* In P. Currah, R. Juang, & S. Minter (Eds.), *Transgender rights.* Minneapolis: University of Minnesota Press.

Grossman, A. H., & D'Augelli, A. R. (2006). Transgender youth: Invisible and vulnerable. *Journal of Homosexuality, 51*(1), 111–128.

Grossman, A. H., & D'Augelli, A. R. (2007). Transgender youth and life-threatening behaviors. *Suicide and Life-Threatening Behaviors, 37,* 527–537.

Grossman, A. H., D'Augelli, A. R., Howell, T. J., & Hubbard, S. (2005). Parents' reactions to transgender youths' gender nonconforming expression and identity. *Journal of Gay & Lesbian Social Services, 18*(1), 3–16.

Guiffrida, D., Gouveia, A., Wall, A., & Seward, D. (2008). Development and validation of the need for relatedness at college questionnaire (NRC-Q). *Journal of Diversity in Higher Education,* *1*(4), 251–261.

Gurin, P., Dey, E. L., Hurtado, S., & Gurin, G. (2002). Diversity and higher education: Theory and impact on educational outcomes. *Harvard Educational Review, 72*(3), 330–367.

Haider-Markel, D. P. (1998). The politics of social regulatory policy: State and federal hate crime policy and implementation effort. *Political Research Quarterly, 51*(1), 69–88.

Hall, R., & Sandler, R. (1984). *Out of the classroom: A chilly campus climate for women?* Washington, DC: Project on the Status and Education of Women, Association of American Colleges.

Harper, S. R., & Hurtado, S. (2007). Nine themes in campus racial climates and implications for institutional transformation. In S. R. Harper & L. D. Patton (Eds.), *Responding to the realities of race on campus* (pp. 7–24). San Francisco: Jossey-Bass.

Harry, J. (1990). Conceptualizing anti-gay violence. *Journal of Interpersonal Violence, 5*(3), 350–358.

Hart, J., & Fellabaum, J. (2008). Analyzing campus climate studies: Seeking to define and understand. *Journal of Diversity in Higher Education, 1*(4), 222–234.

Hiestand, K. R., & Levitt, H. M. (2005). Butch identity development: The formation of an authentic gender. *Feminism & Psychology, 15*(1), 61–85.

Hill, D. B. (2002). Genderism, transphobia, and gender bashing: A framework for interpreting anti-transgender violence. In B. Wallace & R. Carter (Eds.), *Understanding and dealing with violence: A multicultural approach* (pp. 113–136). Thousand Oaks, CA: Sage.

Hill, D. B. (2005). Coming to terms: Using technology to know identity. *Sexuality and Culture, 9*(3), 24–52.

Hirschfeld, M. (1991). *Transvestites: The erotic drive to cross dress* (M. A. Lombardi-Nash, Trans.). Buffalo, NY: Prometheus Books. (Original work published 1910)

Hofstede, G., Neuijen, B., Ohayv, D. D., & Sanders, G. (1990). Measuring organizational cultures: A qualitative and quantitative study across twenty cases. *Administrative Science Quarterly, 35,* 286–316.

Hogan, T. L., & Rentz, A. L. (1996). Homophobia in the academy. *Journal of College Student Development, 37*(3), 309–314.

Hogan-Finlay, M., Spanos, N. P., & Jones, B. (1997). Development of the cross-gender lifestyle: Comparisons of cross-gender men with heterosexual controls. In B. Bullough, V. L. Bullough, & J. Elias (Eds.), *Gender blending* (pp. 161–173). Amherst, NY: Prometheus Books.

Hubbard, R. (1998). Gender and genitals: Constructs of sex and gender. In D. Denny (Ed.), *Current concepts in transgender identity* (pp. 45–54). New York: Garland.

Human Rights Campaign. (2011a). *Employers with domestic partner health benefits.* Retrieved April 24, 2011, from http://www.hrc.org/ issues/workplace.asp

Human Rights Campaign. (2011b). *Employers with non-discrimination policies that include gender identity.* Retrieved April 24, 2011, from http://www.hrc.org/issues/workplace.asp

Human Rights Campaign. (2011c). *Employers with non-discrimination policies that include sexual orientation.* Retrieved April 24, 2011, from http://www.hrc.org/issues/workplace.asp

Hurtado, S. (1992). The campus racial climate: Contexts of conflict. *Journal of Higher Education, 63,* 539–569.

Hurtado, S. (1994). The institutional climate for talented Latino students. *Research in Higher Education, 35*(1), 21–41.

Hurtado, S., & Carter, D. F. (1997). Effects of college transition and perceptions of the campus racial climate on Latino college students' sense of belonging. *Sociology of Education, 70*(4), 324–345.

Hurtado, S., Milem, J. F., Clayton-Pedersen, A. R., & Allen, W. R. (1998). Enhancing campus climates for racial/ethnic diversity: Educational policy and practice. *Review of Higher Education, 21,* 279–302.

Hurtado, S., & Ponjuan, L. (2005). Latino educational outcomes and the campus climate. *Journal of Hispanic Higher Education, 4*(3), 235–251.

James, L., & Jones, A. (1974). Organizational climate: A review of theory and research. *Psychological Bulletin, 81,* 1096–1112.

Janoff-Bulman, R., & Frieze, I. H. (1983). A theoretical perspective for understanding reactions to victimization. *Journal of Social Issues, 39*(2), 1–17.

Johnson, R. B., & Onwuegbuzie, J. (2004). Mixed methods research: A research paradigm whose time has come. *Education Researcher, 33*(7), 14–26.

Kahn, W. A. (1990). Psychological conditions of personal engagement and disengagement at work. *Academy of Management Journal, 33,* 692–724.

Kenagy, G. P. (2005). Transgender health: Findings from two needs assessment studies in Philadelphia. *Health and Social Work, 30,* 19–26.

Kessler, S. J., & McKenna, W. (2006). Toward a theory of gender. In S. Stryker & S. Whittle (Eds.), *The transgender studies reader* (pp. 165–182). New York: Routledge.

Kitzinger, C. (1987). *The social construction of lesbianism.* London: Sage.

Kitzinger, C., & Wilkinson, S. (1995). Transitions from heterosexuality to lesbianism: The discursive production of lesbian identities. *Developmental Psychology, 31,* 95–104.

Kohlberg, L. (1966). A cognitive-developmental analysis of children's sex role concepts and attitudes. In E. E. Maccoby (Ed.), *The development of sex differences* (pp. 82–173). Stanford, CA: Stanford University Press.

Koken, J. A., Bambi, D. S., & Parson, J. T. (2009). Experience of familial acceptance-rejection among transwomen of color. *Journal of Family Psychology, 23,* 853–860.

Korrell, S. C., & Lorah, P. (2007). An overview of affirmative psychotherapy and counseling with transgender clients. In K. J. Bieschke, M. Perez, & K. A. DeBord (Eds.), *Handbook of counseling and psychotherapy with lesbian, gay, bisexual, and transgender clients* (2nd ed., pp. 271–288). Washington, DC: American Psychological Association.

Lawrence, F. M. (1999). *Punishing hate: Bias crimes under American law.* Cambridge, MA: Harvard University Press.

Lev, A. I. (2004). *Transgender emergence: Therapeutic guidelines for working with gender-variant people and their families.* New York: Haworth Clinical Practice Press.

Lewin, E. (1993). Lesbian mothers: Accounts of gender in American culture. New York: Cornell University Press.

Lewins, F. (1995). *Transsexualism in society: A sociology of male-to-female transsexuals.* Melbourne, Australia: Macmillan.

Litwin, G. H., & Stringer, R. A. (1968). *Motivation and organizational climate.* Boston: Graduate School of Business Administration, Harvard University.

Lombardi, E. L., Wilchins, R. A., Priesing, D., & Malouf, D. (2001). Gender violence: Transgender experiences with violence and discrimination. *Journal of Homosexuality, 42*(1), 89–101.

Maass, A., Cadinu, M., Guarnieri, G., & Grasselli, A. (2003). Sexual harassment under social identity threat: The computer harassment paradigm. *Journal of Personality and Social Psychology, 85,* 853–870.

Malaney, G. D., Williams, E. A., & Geller, W. W. (1997). Assessing campus climate for gays, lesbians, and bisexuals at two institutions. *Journal of College Student Development, 38*(4), 365–375.

McCauley, E. A., & Ehrhardt, A. A. (1977). Role expectations and definitions: A comparison of female transsexuals and lesbians. *Journal of Homosexuality, 3*(2), 137–147.

McKinney, J. S. (2005). On the margins: A study of the experiences of transgender college students. *Journal of Gay and Lesbian Issues in Education, 3*(1), 63–76.

Migeon, C. J., Wisniewski, A. B., & Gearhart, J. P. (2001). *Syndromes of abnormal sex differentiation.* Retrieved August 24, 2010, from http://www.med.jhu.edu/pedendo/intersex/sd4.html

Milem, J. F., Chang, M. J., & Antonio, A. L. (2005). *Making diversity work on campus: A research-based perspective.* Washington, DC: Association of American Colleges and Universities.

Money, J. (1993). Sin, sickness, or status? Homosexual gender identity and psychoneuroendrocrinology. In L. D. Garnets & D. C. Kimmel (Eds.), *Psychological perspectives on lesbian and gay experiences* (pp. 131–167). New York: Columbia University Press.

Moran, L. J., & Sharpe, A. N. (2001). Policing the transgender/violence relation. *Current Issues in Criminal Justice, 13*(3), 269–285.

Moran, L. J., & Sharpe, A. N. (2004). Violence, identity, and policing: The case of violence against transgender people. *Criminal Justice, 4,* 395–417.

National Coalition of Anti-Violence Programs [NCAVP]. (2008). *Anti-lesbian, gay, bisexual and transgender violence in 2007: A report of the National Coalition of Anti-Violence Programs.* New York: Author.

National Gay and Lesbian Task Force. (2011a). *Hate crime laws in the U.S.* Retrieved April 24, 2011, from http://www.thetaskforce.org/downloads/reports/issue_maps/hate_crimes_7_09_color.pdf

National Gay and Lesbian Task Force. (2011b). *State nondiscrimination laws in the U.S.* Retrieved April 24, 2011, from http://www.thetaskforce.org/downloads/reports/issue_maps/non_discrimination_7_09_color.pdf

National Gay and Lesbian Task Force & National Center for Transgender Equality [NGLTF/NCTE]. (2009). *The prevalence of discrimination against transgender people: Preliminary findings of a study by the National Center for Transgender Equality and the National Gay and Lesbian Task Force.* Washington, DC: National Center for Transgender Equality. Retrieved December 5, 2009, from http://transequality.org/Resources/NCTE_prelim_survey_econ.pdf

Nelson, E., & Krieger, S. (1997). Changes in attitudes toward homosexuality in college students: Implementation of a gay men and lesbian peer panel. *Journal of Homosexuality, 33*(2), 63–81.

Nestle, J., Howell, C., & Wilchins, R. (Eds.). (2002). *Genderqueer: Voices from beyond the sexual binary.* Los Angeles: Alyson.

Norris, F. H., & Kaniasty, K. (1991). The psychological experience of crime: A test of the mediating role of beliefs in explaining the distress of victims. *Journal of Social and Clinical Psychology, 10,* 239–261.

Norris, W. P. (1992). Liberal attitudes and homophobic acts: The paradoxes of homosexual experience in a liberal institution. *Journal of Homosexuality, 22,* 81–120.

O'Keefe, T., & Fox, K. (Eds.). (2003). *Finding the real me: True tales of sex and gender diversity.* San Francisco: Jossey-Bass.

O'Keefe, T., & Fox, K. (Eds.). (2008). *Trans people in love.* New York: Routledge.

Parker, C. P., Baltes, B. B., Young, S. A., Huff, J. W., Altmann, R. A., Lacost, H. A., & Roberts, J. E. (2003). Relationships between psychological climate perceptions and work outcomes: A meta-analytic review. *Journal of Organizational Behavior, 24,* 389–416.

Person, E., & Ovesey, L. (1974a). The transsexual syndrome in males: I. Primary transsexualism. *American Journal of Psychotherapy, 28,* 4–20.

Person, E., & Ovesey, L. (1974b). The transsexual syndrome in males: II. Secondary transsexualism. *American Journal of Psychotherapy, 28,* 174–193.

Ponse, B. (1978). *Identities in the lesbian world: The social construction of self.* Westport, CT: Greenwood Press.

Prince, V. C. (1962). 166 men in dresses. *Sexology, 3,* 520–525.

Prince, V. C., & Bentler, P. M. (1972). Survey of 504 cases of transvestism. *Psychological Reports, 31*(3), 903–917.

Pusch, R. S. (2005). Objects of curiosity: Transgender college students' perception of the reactions of others. *Journal of Gay and Lesbian Issues in Education, 3*(1), 45–61.

Rachlin, K. (1999). Factors which influence individual's decisions when considering female-to male genital reconstructive surgery. *International Journal of Transgenderism, 3*(3), http://www.symposion.com/ijt/ijt990302.htm

Ragins, B. R., & Cornwell, J. M. (2001). Pink triangles: Antecedents and consequences of perceived workplace discrimination against gay and lesbian employees. *Journal of Applied Psychology, 86,* 1244–1261.

Rankin, S. (2001). *National campus climate for underrepresented people.* Unpublished manuscript.

Rankin, S. R. (2003). *Campus climate for gay, lesbian, bisexual, and transgender people: A national perspective.* New York: National Gay and Lesbian Task Force Policy Institute.

Rankin, S. (2006). LGBTQA students on campus: Is higher education making the grade? *Journal of Gay and Lesbian Issues in Education, 3*(2/3), 111–117.

Rankin, S. (2007). *Experiences of gay men in fraternities: From 1960 to 2007.* Charlotte, NC: Lambda 10 Project.

Rankin, S. R., & Reason, R. D. (2005). Differing perceptions: How students of color and white students perceive campus climate for underrepresented groups. *Journal of College Student Development, 46,* 43–61.

Rankin, S., & Reason, R. (2008). Transformational tapestry model: A comprehensive approach to transforming campus climate. *Journal of Diversity in Higher Education, 1*(4), 262–274.

Rankin, S., & Reason, R. (forthcoming). *Transforming campus climate: Assessment and planning.* Sterling, VA: Stylus.

Reason, R., & Rankin, S. (2006). College students' experiences and perceptions of harassment on campus: An exploration of gender differences. *College Student Affairs Journal, 26*(1), 7–29.

Richardson, D. (1984). The dilemma of essentiality in homosexuality theory. *Journal of Homosexuality, 9,* 79–90.

Ringo, P. (2002). Media roles in female-to-male transsexual and transgender identity formation. *International Journal of Transgenderism.* Retrieved August 24, 2010, from http://www.symposion.com/ijt/ijtv006n003_01.htm

Risser, J. M., Shelton, A., McCurdy, S., Atkinson, J., Padgett, P., & Useche, B. (2005). Sex, drugs, violence, and HIV status among male-to-female transgender persons in Houston, Texas. In W. Bockting & E. Avery (Eds.), *Transgender health and HIV prevention: Needs assessment studies from across the United States* (pp. 67–74). Binghamton, NY: Haworth Medical Press.

Rousseau, D. M. (1988). The construction of climate in organizational research. In C. L. Cooper & I. T. Robertson (Eds.), *International review of industrial and organizational psychology* (pp. 139–158). New York: Wiley.

Rubin, G. (1975). The traffic in women: Notes on the political economy of sex. In R. R. Reither (Ed.), *Toward an anthropology of women* (pp. 157–210). New York: Monthly Review Press.

Rubin, H. (2003). *Self-made men: Identity and embodiment among transsexual men.* Nashville, TN: Vanderbilt University Press.

Rudd, P. J. (1999). *Crossdressing with dignity: The case for transcending gender lines.* Katy, TX: PM Publishers. (Original work published 1990)

Samons, S. L. (2009). *When the opposite sex isn't: Sexual orientation in male-to-female transgender people.* New York: Routledge.

Sánchez, F. J., & Vilain, E. (2009). Collective self-esteem as a coping resource for male-to-female transsexuals. *Journal of Counseling Psychology, 56,* 202–209.

Sapir, E. (1949). *Selected writings in language, culture and personality.* Berkeley: University of California Press.

Schott, R. L. (1995). The childhood and family dynamics of transvestites. *Archives of Sexual Behavior, 24*(3), 309–327.

Scott-Dixon, K. (Ed.). (2006). *Trans/forming feminism: Trans/feminist voices speak out.* Toronto, Canada: Sumach Press.

Sears, J. T., & Williams, W. L. (Eds.). (1997). *Overcoming heterosexism and homophobia: Strategies that work.* New York: Columbia University Press.

Settles, I. H., Cortina, L. M., Malley, J., & Stewart, A. J. (2006). The climate for women in academic science: The good, the bad, and the changeable. *Psychology of Women Quarterly, 30,* 47–58.

Shapiro, E. (2004). Trans'cending barriers: Transgender organizing on the Internet. *Journal of Gay and Lesbian Social Services, 16*(3/4), 165–179.

Shapiro, E. (2010). *Gender circuits: Bodies and identities in a technological age.* New York: Routledge.

Silverschanz, P., Cortina, L., Konik, J., & Magley, V. (2008). Slurs, snubs, and queer jokes: Incidence and impact of heterosexist harassment in academia. *Sex Roles, 58,* 179–191.

Smith, D. G., Gerbrick, G., Figueroa, M., Watkins, G., Levitan, T., Moore, L., Merchant, P., Beliak, H., & Figueroa, B. (1997). *Diversity works: The emerging picture of how students benefit.* Washington, DC: Association of American Colleges and Universities.

Smith, G. A. (2000). *Transgender day of remembrance.* Retrieved August 24, 2010, from http://www.gender.org/remember/index.html

Stekel, W. (1930). *Sexual aberrations: The phenomenon of fetishism in relation to sex* (S. Parker, Trans.). New York: Liveright. (Original work published 1922)

Stoller, R. J. (1971). The term "transvestism." *Archives of General Psychiatry, 24,* 230–237.

Stoller, R. J. (1985). *Presentations of gender.* New Haven, CT: Yale University Press.

Stotzer, R. (2008). Gender identity and hate crimes: Violence against transgender people in Los Angeles County. *Sexuality Research & Social Policy, 5*(1), 43–52.

Stotzer, R. L. (2009). Violence against transgender people: A review of the United States data. *Aggression and Violent Behavior, 14,* 170–179.

Stryker, S. (2008). *Transgender history.* Berkeley, CA: Seal Press.

Talamini, J. T. (1982). *Boys will be girls: The hidden world of the heterosexual male transvestite.* Washington, DC: University Press of America.

Tomlinson, M. J., & Fassinger, R. E. (2003). Career development, lesbian identity development and campus climate among lesbian college students. *Journal of College Student Development, 44,* 845–860.

Tong, R. (1998). *Feminist thought.* Boulder, CO: Westview Press.

Transgender Law and Policy Institute. (2011a). *Colleges and universities.* Retrieved April 24, 2011, from http://www.transgenderlaw.org/college/index.htm

Transgender Law and Policy Institute. (2011b). *Colleges and universities with nondiscrimination policies that include gender identity/expression.* Retrieved April 24, 2011, from http://www .transgenderlaw.org/college/index.htm#policies

Transsexual Roadmap. (2010). *Glossary of transgender terms.* Retrieved August 24, 2010, from http://www.tsroadmap.com/start/ tgterms.html

Troiden, R. R. (1989). The formation of homosexual identities. *Journal of Homosexuality, 17*(1/2), 43–73.

Valentine, D. (2007). *Imagining transgender: An ethnography of a category.* Durham, NC: Duke University Press.

Vertinsky, P. (1990). *The eternally wounded woman: Women, doctors and exercise in the late nineteenth century.* Manchester, U.K.: Manchester University Press.

Waldo, C. (1998). Out on campus: Sexual orientation and academic climate in a university context. *American Journal of Community Psychology, 26*(5), 745–774.

Weston, K. (1997). *Families we choose: Lesbians, gays, and kinship.* New York: Columbia University Press.

Wilchins, R. A. (1997). *Read my lips: Sexual subversion and the end of gender.* Ithaca, NY: Firebrand Books.

Wilchins, R. A. (2002). Deconstructing trans. In J. Nestle, C. Howell, & R. A. Wilchins (Eds.), *Genderqueer: Voices from beyond the sexual binary* (pp. 53–63). Los Angeles: Alyson Books.

Wilson, B. E., & Reiner, W. G. (1999). Management of intersex: A shifting paradigm. In A. D. Dreger (Ed.), *Intersex in the age of ethics.* Hagerston, MD: University Publishing Group.

Witten, T. M., & Eyler, A. E. (1999). Hate crimes and violence against the transgendered. *Peace Review: A Journal of Social Justice, 11,* 461–468.

Wolf-Wendel, L. E., Toma, J. D., & Morphew, C. C. (2001). How much difference is too much difference? Perceptions of gay men and lesbians in intercollegiate athletics. *Journal of College Student Development, 42,* 465–479.

Wood, J. (1997). *Gendered lives: Communication, gender and culture* (2nd ed.). Belmont, CA: Wadsworth Press.

Worthington, R. L., Navarro, R. L., Loewy, M., & Hart, J. (2008). Color-blind racial attitudes, social dominance orientation, racial-ethnic group membership and college students' perceptions of campus climate. *Journal of Diversity in Higher Education, 1*(1), 8–19.

Xavier, J. (2006). *The Washington, D.C. transgender needs-assessment survey: Final report for phase two.* Washington, DC: Gender Education and Advocacy. Retrieved August 24, 2010, from http://www.gender.org/resources/dge/gea01011.pdf

Xavier, J. M., Bobbin, M., Singer, B., & Budd, E. (2005). A needs assessment of transgendered people of color living in Washington, DC. *International Journal of Transgenderism, 8*(2/3), 31–47.

INDEX

Italics indicate pages with tables.

data analysis. *See* statistical analyses

D'Augelli, Anthony, 53–54, 60–61

definitions, in general, 198–199n2. *See also specific terms*

demographics of survey participants, 21–36; age, 29–30; challenges, physical/emotional/cognitive, 35–36; gender expression, 27–28, *28*; gender identity, 22–23, *24, 25,* 25–27; interview protocol, 181–182; race, 30, *31*; sex, 22, *22*; sexual orientation, 30–35, *34*; statistical analysis, 185–186, *186, 187*; survey questions about, 171–173

denial: overcoming, 122, 131–132; of uncertainty about one's gender, 50–51

depression, 36

Devor, Aaron, 47–48, 113–114, 120, 123, 124

Diagnostic and Statistical Manual of Mental Disorders (American Psychiatric Association), 5

dichotomy in language, 17

"different gender": as identity, feeling and expressing, 148; as term, ix, 27. *See also* gender-queer (GQ)

disability: defined, 170; survey participant demographics, 35–36

disorders of sex development (DSD), 15, 19, 198n1

diversity, transgender, viii–ix, 4–5

Docter, Richard, 43, 143–144, 146

Doe v. Yunits (2000), xiii, 197n1 (foreword)

Ebaugh, Helen Rose Fuchs, 113

educational success and campus climate, 83–84

Ehrhardt, Anke, 3

Ekins, Richard, 113

Elshtain, Jean, 17

emotional challenges/disabilities, 35–36

emotional reaction to gender difference, 43–45

employment discrimination. *See* job discrimination

environments, hostile, 90–94

experiences: of gender difference, 43–45, 75; of harassment and violence, 96–97; redefining, 5–7; statistical analysis of responses, *187–188,* 188, *189–190,* 190, *191*; survey questions about, 178–180

extended family, coming out to, 65, *67*

Eyler, Evan, 93

family, coming out to, 65, *66, 67. See also* parents, coming out to

fears, physical safety, 98–99

Feinberg, Leslie, 149

Felsenthal, Kim, 93

female gender identity: feeling and expressing, 126–128; repressing or hiding, 128–129

hormones, taking: by female-to-male/transgender individuals, 122–123; by male-to-female/transgender individuals, 132
hostile environments, 90–94
Hubbard, Ruth, 18, 19
Hurtado, Sylvia, 82, 83, 87
hypermasculinity, flight into by male-to-female/transgender individuals, 129

identity, gender. *See* gender identity
infants, "corrective" surgery for, 18, 19
Internet, importance of, 57–59, 75, 121, 140–141
interviews: about, 9–10, 11; demographic information, 181–182; questions, 183
intimidation, avoiding by concealing one's identity, 99–101

job discrimination: about, xii–xiii, 101–103; and age, 103–104; and campus climate, 87–88; genderqueer issues, 155; and level of outness, 104–105; and male-to-female/transgender individuals, 136; and political activism, 64; and race, 105–106; and sexual orientation, 104
Jorgensen, Christine, 55, 130

Kessler, Suzanne, 18
Kohlberg, Lawrence, 42
Korell, Shannon Chavez, 35

language: of anti-transgender bias, 89; cultural values in, 16–17, 199n3 (chap. 1); dichotomy in, 17; of gender, 16–18; of gender identity, 23, *24*, *25*, 25–26, 165–166; inclusive, 6; of sexual orientation, 33
learning about other transsexual people, 121–122, 129–130, 140
lesbian, female-to-male/transgender initially identifying as, 51–52, 118–120. *See also* LGBT people, campus climate for; LGBT/transgender communities
Lev, Arlene Istar, 114
Levitt, Heidi, 8
Lewins, Frank, 111, 112, 113
LGBT people, campus climate for, 84–87
LGBT/transgender communities: creating a home within or outside of, 154–155; not fitting in with, 153–154
limitations of study, 11–12
Lorah, Peggy, 35

"Mahu," as term, 199n1 (chap. 2)
male gender identity: feeling and expressing, 117; repressing or hiding, 117–118
male-to-different-gender (MTDG): coming out to others, *65*, *66*, *67*, *68*; cross-dressers compared to, ix–x; defined, ix, 27; socializing with other transgender people, 61–62

"transvestites," as term, 2, 3, 6.
  See also cross-dressers (CD);
  cross-dressing (CD)
Tri-Ess (Society for the Second
  Self), 140, 144
Troiden, Richard, 10
Turner, Louisa, 112

university climate. *See* campus
  climate
urban residents, 60–61

values, language as expression
  of, 16–17, 199n3 (chap. 1)
violence. *See* harassment and
  violence

Waldo, Craig, 88
Washington, DC, 92–93
wholeness, sense of, 125–126,
  136–137
Williams, Walter, 84, 85–86

Witten, Tarynn, 93
wives: of cross-dressers, 143–
  145; of male-to-female/trans-
  gender individuals, 134–136
women, transsexual. *See* male-to-
  female/transgender (MTF/T);
  male-to-female/transgender
  (MTF/T) milestones
Wood, Julia, 17
work, flight into by male-to-
  female/transgender individuals, 129
workplace discrimination. *See*
  job discrimination

youth, transgender: gender difference, experience of, 44–45;
  identity formation among,
  160–163; murder of, 92

"ze," as gender-neutral pronoun,
  197n2